THE WYCLIFFE FILE

Wycliffe

The Magnificent Five: (l to r) Dixon, Lane, Wycliffe, Kersey and Potter

THE WYCLIFFE FILE

Wycliffe

The story of the ITV detective series

GEOFF TIBBALLS

BXTREE

ACKNOWLEDGEMENTS

The author would like to thank the following for their help and friendly co-operation in the preparation of this book: Mike Alsford, Laura Aviles, Adam Barker, Mike Bartley, Sue Bide, Sarah Bird, John Burley, Trevor Colman, Jon Day, Roger Elliott, Martyn Friend, Sara Hamill, Aaron Harris, Dee Hellier, Andrew Jack, Gavin James, Alison Mackinnon, Helen Masters, Steve Matthews, Nick Middleton, Geraint Morris, Lamorna Penrose, Reg Samuel, Jack Shepherd, Penny Simpson, Kathrine Smith, Steve Trafford, Tim Vaughan, Susanna Wadeson, Tim Wylton, Jimmy Yuill.

First published in Great Britain in 1995 by Boxtree Limited

Text © Geoff Tibballs/Boxtree Ltd 1995

Photographs © HTV 1995

Photography by Mike Alsford

1 3 5 7 9 10 8 6 4 2

Designed by Martin Lovelock

Printed and bound in the UK by Cambus Litho Ltd for

Boxtree Limited

Broadwall House · 21 Broadwall · London SE1 9PL

Reprographics by Jade Reprographics, Braintree, Essex.

A CIP catalogue entry for this book is available from the British Library.

ISBN 0 75221 001 7

Front and back cover photographs by Mike Alsford

CONTENTS

THE GAS MAN COMETH

It was in 1967 when, after working twenty years with the Gas Board and another twenty as a biology teacher, Cornishman John Burley set out to create a detective character to supplement his future pension. His name was Charles Wycliffe (pronounced Wickliff) and, in 1993, at the ripe old age of seventy-nine, John Burley finally saw his literary creation transfer to television. It was a dream come true.

'I never thought I would get Wycliffe on to television – never in a million years,' says the author who has so far written twenty books about the Cornish detective under the name of W.J. Burley. 'I just didn't think they were dramatic enough. I didn't think they had enough punch and thought they relied too much on the presentation of personalities. My publishers, Gollancz, had always said to me that if I had ambitions about getting Wycliffe on to television, I should get an agent. But I never bothered.

'I heard the odd rumour that a television company was interested in my novels but to tell the truth I didn't think anything more about it. Then one day I was sitting in front of my word processor writing my latest Wycliffe book when the telephone rang. It was Steve Matthews, the Director of Programmes at HTV.'

Steve Matthews had been looking for a West Country detective to do for that region what Inspector Morse had done for Oxford and Bergerac had done for Jersey. It was he who spotted John Burley's Wycliffe books and thought they had considerable potential.

John recalls: 'He invited my wife Muriel and me up to Bristol and said that he wanted to make a pilot programme which, if successful, would lead to a series in 1994. I was absolutely astonished but didn't take much persuading. At my time of life, something like this is simply a wonderful bonus.'

One of nature's true gentlemen, John has lived in Cornwall all his life and his Cornish roots go back at least five generations on both sides of his family. He was born in Falmouth at the outbreak of the First World War and had what he describes as a 'strict Wesleyan upbringing.' When he was twelve years old, he read Conan Doyle's Sherlock Holmes stories and they fuelled his ambition to write.

Growing up in 1920s Falmouth, he had first-hand experience of a murder case. 'A local girl didn't want to have sex with a boy who lived across the road from me, so he strangled her with a scarf. A lot of the local women said she was asking for it, but he was lucky not to be hanged and ended up serving thirteen years in jail. I knew him before and after the murder but never mentioned it. It was a subject everybody just ignored.'

John Burley on location

Assisted by Muriel, the teenage sweetheart who later became his wife, John began writing short stories which he then offered to magazines. But, disheartened by the rejection letters, he temporarily abandoned his writing ambitions and opted for the security of a job as a gas engineer.

'I was with the Gas Board for twenty years, including during the Second World War when I helped provide gas for a secret radar factory. When the industry was nationalized, I hated it and left to go to university.'

At the age of thirty-six, he won a Mature State Scholarship to Balliol

College, Oxford, to read zoology. 'We were very poor while I was studying. At home, there was no water, electricity or gas and when I was away at college, Muriel and our boys, Alan and Nigel, were living off what food they could pick up locally, mainly cod and rabbit.'

After obtaining his degree, he taught biology at Newquay and at Richmond Grammar School in Surrey, only to discover that, because he was a late entrant into the teaching profession, he would only receive a small pension on his eventual retirement. Realizing that he would have insufficient funds to see himself and Muriel through their twilight years, he decided to pursue a secondary career and naturally his thoughts returned to writing.

'The Georges Simenon novels and in particular the 'Maigret' television series starring Rupert Davies had rekindled my enthusiasm for detective stories so while I was teaching by day, I started writing by night. To my delight and surprise, I had my first novel, *A Taste of Power*, published by Gollancz in 1966. The hero was a private detective called Henry Pym who was a bit like Lord Peter Wimsey. I based many of the characters on people I had known from teaching. I killed off an English teacher I'd never much cared for and made an old maths teacher the murderer! It was great fun being able to indulge myself like that without anybody knowing.

Wycliffe and his team prepare to tackle another case

'My director of education read it and realized he was in it too, with all his bad habits. He came up to me and said, "You bastard!" and I thought I was in for the high jump, but he didn't really mind and took it in good part.

'The success of that made me want to write another book but I didn't think Henry Pym had much of a shelf life. So I set about creating a new central character, this time a police

8

detective. I knew that the name would be all-important. I had always admired the name Maigret – it's evocative, it's not common and it's the sort of name you don't forget in a hurry. Flicking through possible candidates, my mind settled on John Wycliffe, the translator of the Bible in the fourteenth century. I felt the name Wycliffe had the same qualities as Maigret and a touch of class.'

John's first Wycliffe book, *The Mystery of the Three Toes Pussy*, was published in 1968. His twentieth, *Wycliffe and the House of Fear*, has just been published. Although he is not as well known as Colin Dexter, Ruth Rendell or P.D. James, his books have built up a loyal following.

'The books have always sold quite well in America,' says John, 'and have been translated into German, French, Swedish, Dutch and Italian. In monetary terms, I certainly haven't made a fortune but it has been a living for us since I retired from teaching in 1974.'

The construction of the Wycliffe thrillers is very much a joint effort between John and Muriel, his wife of fifty-seven years. 'We sit down together and start by choosing character names and a setting. Gradually, we build up a group of people and work out their personalities, backgrounds and so on. I usually write about thirty pages of characterizations and then, when all that's in place, I decide who's going to be murdered and who the killer will be. You see, to me, characters and settings are all-important. I allow the plot to develop from them. I've never been systematic enough to work out the plot first.'

In fact, John writes the way Wycliffe investigates. He soaks up the location, comes to terms with the people and only then worries about the plot. 'Crime writers,' says John, 'suffer from having to have a plot without being able to characterize their people too strongly. Otherwise it becomes evident who the murderer is likely to be.

'I'm very fond of Wycliffe. He's a caring, compassionate man with high morals. He is always fighting his conscience, the result of having had the same sort of restricted upbringing as I did. I suppose he is the sort of character I'd have been if I had ever become a policeman. Not that there was much chance of that – I wouldn't have liked the discipline of the police force, although I would have enjoyed the detective work.

'Wycliffe's first assistant was Inspector Gill, but then Kersey came along a little later. Franks was there from the start – the epitome of the jolly pathologist – and Potter and Dixon arrived around 1976. In my books, Potter has a big paunch while Dixon is tall and thin so they set each other off nicely. Lucy Lane was introduced in 1985 in the story *The Four Jacks*. It was at a time when women were making their presence felt in the police force and I felt I ought to reflect that. When I started Wycliffe in the Sixties, women never really progressed beyond the rank of WPC.'

John is full of praise for the TV cast of 'Wycliffe', especially Jack Shepherd. 'He is the kind of actor I'd have picked to play Wycliffe. He is a very intelligent man and my wife and I say that when we talk to Jack, he's often more like Wycliffe off screen than on! He has that deliberate, thoughtful way of speaking which makes him ideal for the role.

'My books have been changed quite a bit for television although they're still recognizably my books. Some of the plot lines were

The shoot-out at the climax to 'The Scapegoat' was created specially for the television adaptation

altered in the first series and in the episode "The Pea Green Boat", the murderer was a totally different character! And whilst there's not much nudity or explicit sex in my books, what there is they cut out.

'I remember when they were filming "The Scapegoat", they phoned and asked me whether I wanted to come out to watch the big shoot-out at the end.

'I said: "There isn't a shoot-out in that story."

'They replied: "There is now!"

'Having said that, I realize how difficult my books are to adapt for television. Looking at the six they did in the first series, I felt they missed the point sometimes but I could understand why they did it. I didn't think much of the pilot episode but they then hotted the stories up and I think they made good television. For this second series, none of the eight episodes are adaptations – they are all fresh stories based on my characters. Far from being offended, I am happier they are doing it this way.

'Obviously the television series is more forceful than the books with less time and room for characterization. But I don't mind. It helps to sell my books and I can still write my Wycliffe as I see him.'

John insists that his latter-day fame will not change his lifestyle. 'I don't really have much of life left to change,' he jokes. 'We still live in the same three-bedroom bungalow overlooking the coast in the Cornish hamlet of Holywell, near Newquay, that I bought for £1,850 in 1957 when it was the only place we could afford. Now for the first time in my life, I no longer have to worry about money.

'We never go on holiday. I still love Cornwall even though I can remember the days when there were fewer tourists about and you could roam the beautiful countryside in perfect solitude. Now you can only do that in winter.

'I still work four hours every day, lubricated by *Liebfraumilch*, and, although both my sons have now retired, I have no plans to follow suit. I will keep going as long as my health holds out. It's wonderful that all this has happened to me even though I have to be realistic and accept that if "Wycliffe" were to run as long as, say, "Inspector Morse", I probably wouldn't be around to see it.'

WYCLIFFE AND THE TELEVISION ADAPTATION

The man entrusted with the task of transferring John Burley's Wycliffe books to television was double award-winning producer Geraint Morris, the force behind such hugely successful series as 'Softly, Softly', 'The Onedin Line', 'Juliet Bravo' and 'Casualty'.

After studying at Cardiff College of Music and Drama, Geraint joined the BBC in 1963. He says: 'I was one of those lucky ones that joined to make the tea and ended up as a producer!'

At that time the BBC had two popular but extremely different police series – steady old 'Dixon of Dock Green', which had been running (or rather walking at a leisurely pace) since 1955, and the brash newcomer 'Z Cars'.

'As far as British police shows were concerned, "Z Cars" broke the mould,' says Geraint. 'It showed coppers doing a difficult job and showed them as real people, having a sense of humour. But above all, it didn't pull any punches and often showed policemen as being less than perfect. I came into that team in 1968 with "Softly, Softly", a "Z Cars" spin-off which had been set up two years earlier to recognize the formation of regional crime squads.'

'Z Cars' and 'Softly, Softly' put the emphasis very much on realism and aimed to reflect the mood of the day whereas, says Geraint, 'dear old George Dixon was still saying things at the end of each programme which made us believe that the Krays didn't exist.'

By 1971, Geraint had graduated to directing 'Softly, Softly' and from 1973 until 1976 was the series' producer. In 1977, during his four years as producer/director of 'The Onedin Line' (part of which was filmed in Falmouth), he left the BBC to go freelance. 'I felt I wanted to spread my wings,' he says. Following a spell producing 'Juliet Bravo', he launched and later revamped the highly acclaimed 'Casualty', in between times serving a year as producer of 'The Bill'. In 1992, he collected the Royal Television Society's Best Series award for 'Casualty' and the following year won the RTS Best Regional Programme award for 'Selected Exits'.

'Wycliffe' producer
Geraint Morris

It was in 1993 that Geraint was approached by Huw Davies, the Group Director of Television for HTV.

'He came to me after HTV had made the pilot of "Wycliffe" and asked if I was willing and able to come and make a six-part series of "Wycliffe" for them. I was working as a drama producer for Red Rooster Film and Television Entertainment at the time, so we made the series together.'

But before that stage could be reached, there was much work to be done. In the wake of the pilot programme, screened in the summer of 1993, the ITV Network Centre had ordered more action and no domestic scenes. There was a wholesale shake-up. The only survivors from the pilot were Jack Shepherd and Cornwall.

One of Geraint Morris's first moves was to bring in Tim Vaughan, who had worked with him on 'The Bill', as script editor. When it comes to police series, there are few finer pedigrees than Tim Vaughan's. In 1988, he had set up the twice-weekly episodes of 'The Bill' and in 1992 had done the same for the award-winning 'Between the Lines'. He has subsequently worked on two series of 'A Touch of Frost' starring David Jason.

The first series of 'Wycliffe' was commissioned in November 1993 with filming due to begin in March so John Burley's books had to be adapted for television very quickly. Tim turned to writers with whom he had previously worked. Steve Trafford, Rob Heyland and Russell Lewis had each won the Writers' Guild Award for the original series of 'Between the Lines' and Steve and

Martyn Friend directs a
robed John McEnery in
'The Scapegoat'

Russell had both also written for 'The Bill'; Edward Canfor-Dumas had penned fifteen episodes of 'The Bill'; and Andrew Holden had worked with Tim on 'Emmerdale Farm', as it was then known, before becoming story editor on 'EastEnders'. Between them, they read all of John Burley's Wycliffe books.

'We had to have a long rein to adapt them,' says Tim. 'John Burley's books are very theatrical, slightly macabre and with plenty of Gothic images. They are wonderful on settings and characters – isolated communities peopled with eccentrics and lots of "tarts with a heart". But they are really difficult to translate for television, particularly since we had to have them written in six to eight weeks. So we had to re-interpret the books. I'd find an image here, a thought there and use those. I aimed to create something that was part thriller, part black comedy. Some stories, like "The Four Jacks", remained fairly faithful to the original but with others, I'm afraid we did take a few liberties. For example when we were hunting for locations, we found Frontier City, this wild-west theme town, and thought it would be great to end one of the stories with a shoot-out there. So we incorporated that into the climax of "The Scapegoat". Other things, like the body of the old lady in the freezer in "The Tangled Web", are pure Burley.

'Although the order was for a detective series set in Cornwall rather than an adaptation, if we'd had more time, I'm sure we could have stuck to the books more faithfully.'

Steve Trafford, who has also written episodes for 'Emmerdale', 'Medics' and 'Heartbeat', adds: 'We did sometimes have to take John Burley's ideas and change them around a bit. In "The Pea Green Boat", we even changed the murderer! In the book, the killer was a guy with a badly-scarred face who adopted a false identity and returned to wreak a terrible revenge. That worked fine in book form but it wouldn't have worked on television because everyone at home would take one look at his face and immediately say, "He must be the killer." And the aim of any television whodunit is to keep the identity of the murderer a mystery right up until the final scenes. So we had to re-do that story, introducing a couple of new characters. But at the same time, it was a great story to do because of that wonderful visual opening with the exploding boat.

'Similarly, in the book, *The Dead Flautist*, Lander the solicitor collects antiquarian photographs rather than pornography. We introduced the fact that the girl was an aspiring model to update the story, to make it more contemporary. You have to remember that many of the books were written twenty or twenty-five years ago. It was a different world then. We also changed the motive in our version of "The Dead Flautist". In the book, the motive was that the killer had been having a relationship with a woman who had become pregnant. But that motive had already been used in another book we were adapting so we wanted something different. Consequently we came up with the idea that he thought the woman had given him HIV which, of course, is a disease that was unheard of when John wrote the book.'

Steve, who has also written for the second series of 'Wycliffe', concludes: 'My aim with adapting the books was to produce a tight whodunit. I wanted to devise a puzzle and to go on a journey with the police who are trying to solve the puzzle. I was also very aware of the visual demands, the need for plenty of exterior scenes to show the Cornish landscape. So I set out to cut the quiet beauty of Cornwall against the tension and danger in the story.'

The police search for clues in 'The Tangled Web'

Having worked on so many police series, Tim Vaughan had good contacts within the force. He regularly spoke to policemen to ensure authenticity and relied heavily on the input of the police adviser on 'Wycliffe', a serving, middle-ranking officer with CID experience. As a result, a portrait of the fictional force and its characters was drawn up. This 'bible' would form the basis for all 'Wycliffe' storylines and would prove invaluable to the writers.

'Wycliffe' is set in the area covered by the 'A' Division of the fictional South-West Constabulary which is responsible for policing Devon and Cornwall. The Constabulary is divided into six divisions of which 'A' is the farthest south-west. 'A' Division comprises five sub-divisions – Newquay, Truro, Penwith, Penryn and Camborne (where the divisional headquarters are located) – and also covers the Isles of Scilly.

'A' Division is policed by 430 officers, scattered unevenly around the region. Detective Superintendent Wycliffe is the Senior Investigations Officer. It is a vast area to police and a long way from key locations. Wycliffe's supervising officers are some 120 miles to the north-east; the police pathologist, Franks, is based in Plymouth – an hour and a half's drive away; and the forensic laboratories are on the other side of the Severn Estuary, in Chepstow.

Consequently, Cornish police officers are acutely aware of distance. They know, for example, how long it takes to get to the forensic labs and how long the people there will take to get a result. Nevertheless, the PACE (Police and Criminal Evidence) regulations which govern the length of time for which prisoners can be held, are the same as in the rest of the country.

About 200,000 people live permanently in the area but every summer the population increases enormously since Devon and Cornwall attract six million visitors a year. As 'A' Division's ground is the most isolated, quaint and picturesque, many tourists wander through it. Thus crime levels can rise alarmingly and travelling around becomes more difficult due to heavy traffic congestion.

The south-west is also steeped in folklore. Some isolated communities may have adopted the conveniences of a modern lifestyle but still live by their own unique principles. This can be ostracizing to the outsider and can hinder criminal investigation since there is a tendency to close ranks.

Wycliffe heads a team that can be taken from a pool of up to a hundred officers. The size of team depends on the job in hand. When major incidents such as murder take place, Wycliffe and his team have to billet themselves at the nearest divisional or sub-divisional station. They will set up an incident room, perhaps using the village hall, but always rely on the expertise and local knowledge of the 'host' police station. Teamwork and trust is therefore essential, not just between Wycliffe and Inspectors Kersey and Lane, but also between them and the local police officers.

Wycliffe supervises the activities of various investigating teams, each of which is led by an Inspector. For instance, one team gets a profile on the victim by interviewing relatives and friends; another is responsible for house-to-house inquiries and witness statements; another homes in on possible suspects as and when they emerge. Most of this work is shared by Kersey and Lane. Throughout the series, Wycliffe is in on most of the key interviews at the start and finish of the inquiry and also follows up other aspects such as forensic and pathology.

In John Burley's books, Wycliffe hails from Liverpool but, in order to accommodate Jack Shepherd's Leeds accent, it was decided to make him a Yorkshireman for television. He was also reduced in rank from Chief Superintendent in the books to Superintendent.

Geraint Morris explains: 'Our police adviser told us that in reality a Chief Superintendent would these days spend most of his time behind a desk. We wanted Wycliffe to be involved in the actual investigations, to be there at the sharp end of the case. So we demoted him to Superintendent so that he could be in the action more and get his hands a bit dirty.'

Charles Wycliffe is in his late forties, married, with two teenage children – a son and a daughter. He lives in a village outside Camborne, on the north-west coast of Cornwall. He spent part of his childhood in Liverpool but his formative years were in Leeds. His father was a farmer whose drinking and aggression has given

Wycliffe a life-long hatred of violence and pubs. His father committed suicide when Wycliffe was nine by shooting himself with a twelve-bore shotgun. It is something Wycliffe would rather forget. His mother Irene is still alive.

Wycliffe graduated in politics, philosophy and economics from Leeds University where he met his wife Helen. He spent the best part of his twenties as a teacher but an increasing dissatisfaction with the teaching profession led him into policing in the late 1970s. Helen is still a teacher, now headmistress of a middle school in Redruth.

Wycliffe started as a bobby on the toughest streets of Leeds where the PCs walked in pairs, arm in arm down the Headrow and New Briggate on Friday nights. It was here that his abilities as a Rugby League player came in useful. He remains a keen League enthusiast, but from the terraces rather than on the field.

As a result of his education, Wycliffe always was a fast-track officer and quickly made it into CID. A taste for the hectic life took him to London for a spell and by the time he worked for the Metropolitan Police in the early Eighties, he had risen to the rank of Detective Inspector.

He served his apprenticeship in the days before Sir Robert Mark, when the force was renowned for corruption and bad practice. In fact, it was the popular image of the 'bent copper' which prompted Wycliffe to join up. He joined with the best of motives – determined not to be corrupted by 'canteen culture', the rolled-up trouser leg or the 'firm within the firm'. He earned himself a reputation as a straight copper but he was never a 'copper's copper'. It could be that his refusal to conform to some of the less acceptable police stereotypes in his earlier years has prevented him from going further than Detective Superintendent.

Wycliffe transferred to South-West Constabulary to opt out of the Met. rat-race. Cornwall was always Helen and the children's favourite holiday destination and Wycliffe loves sea-fishing. But being a senior investigations officer in a place as large as Cornwall has its drawbacks. It hasn't turned out to be the easier life he and Helen had envisaged. The job frequently means that he has to pack his bags and not see Helen and the kids for days at a time. As a devoted family man, this is not something he enjoys.

Wycliffe is a highly intelligent, instinctive policeman. He has developed a manner, used with his fellow officers as well as suspects, of quiet persistence. He rarely finds it necessary to raise his voice and is a text-book interrogator, firmly believing in PACE and being keenly aware of the prisoner's rights. He knows that the best way to get a suspect to talk is by gentle coaxing rather than strong-arm tactics.

Wycliffe (Jack Shepherd), Lane (Helen Masters) and Kersey (Jimmy Yuill)

With his colleagues, Wycliffe is a believer in open administration and rarely feels the need to pull rank on Kersey and Lane. He demands, and gets, loyalty and dedication from both of them, but is surprisingly liberal and sensitive to their needs. Above all, Wycliffe enjoys his work. Having been disappointed as a 'career copper', all his ambitions are now thrown into solving crime. He loves nothing better than getting his nose into a case and following it through to the end. But he is not too dedicated to be able to relax, to take time off when he needs it and he insists that his colleagues do likewise. He is confident and on top of the job and believes that the detective who labours too long into the night is not only failing his own life and family, but failing the job too.

Wycliffe has no personal hang-ups. He doesn't drink too much, smoke, gamble or chase women. As befits his rank and position, he is avuncular, quiet and authoritative within the office. At home, however, he is relaxed and sociable, throwing himself into whatever family activities are on offer. In short, he is what his own father never was to him – a model parent, and a model husband.

Detective Inspector Doug Kersey is in his late thirties and single. He is from Exeter, an only child whose parents are now dead. On leaving school at sixteen, he joined the army but left after the horrific experience of the Falklands campaign to join the police. Kersey feels confident within the disciplined framework of the police. He knows what is expected of him and is a good,

Aaron Harris (left) and Adam Barker among the ranks of clothes in the wardrobe department

instinctive detective. Wycliffe and he trust each other implicitly. Kersey is untidy and slightly disorganized but Wycliffe and the team find his courage invaluable during times of confrontation.

The only thing Kersey is frightened of is emotional commitment. He goes through the motions of chatting up women, mainly to prove that he's one of the lads. Although sometimes lonely, he is happier living a rootless existence with the job as security and any pub as his social life.

From St. Ives, Detective Inspector Lucy Lane is thirty years old and single. She has always been an ambitious high-achiever, pushed by her parents who are teachers. Lane has a degree in psychology from Bristol University which has helped her meteoric rise in the police. In contrast to Kersey, Lane is a thinker, meticulous in both her work and appearance. She is completely up-to-date with the latest criminal psychology theories and, much to Kersey's irritation, is able to empathize with suspects as well as victims. In many ways, Lane's academic approach makes her closer to Wycliffe than the others. She values his experience and is always keen to learn from him.

The predominantly male investigation teams may have been suspicious of an attractive, ambitious female detective but Lane commands respect. She and Kersey have come to understand both their own and one another's qualities. Wycliffe knows they compliment each other well.

Lane relaxes through sport – mainly running and horse riding. She has considered going to the Met. but she loves the south-west and, for the time being, is fulfilled by her role in the team.

Detective Sergeant Andy Dixon is in his thirties and comes from an army family. He lives with a divorcee and her son. Dixon is good at, and happy to do, the routine work but feels he should be more successful. He does everything he can to get on but keeps being passed over for promotion. The team now suspects that he employs a lot of flashbacks where the action suddenly goes back ten years. Again, that is difficult to accommodate on television.'

The script editor on the second series of 'Wycliffe' is Kathrine Smith who has previously worked on the ITV drama '99 to 1' starring Leslie Grantham. 'Steve Trafford is contributing three of the eight episodes,' says Kathrine, 'and we're also using women writers for the first time, including Isabelle Grey who has worked on "The Bill" but is new to the sixty-minute format.

'One of the things we did after the first series was talk to the regular actors to see how they wanted their characters to develop. Helen Masters was keen for Lane to have something of a private life. There was a lot of speculation during the first run that Lane would be romantically involved with either Wycliffe or Kersey. To discourage that, we have decided to give Lane a boyfriend this time, a freelance journalist called Simon. So she will no longer be seen as the ice maiden career woman. At first, she is worried in case having a journalist boyfriend will affect her job. Then gradually she relaxes and becomes more interested in him until he compromises her position by leaking confidential information.

'Jimmy Yuill was responsible for suggesting that Kersey had an army background and served in the Falklands before going into the police. In an episode in the new series, we have a scene where

Sean Chapman and Cathryn Harrison in 'All for Love'

they have set up an incident room in an army hall. On the wall is a roll of honour board from the Falklands and this causes Kersey to open up about his traumatic experiences in the South Atlantic.

'That is how we will bring out the characters' private lives by including little personal references in the case of the week. It is really quite a challenge to portray personal lives without actually showing a character's home life. For example, there is a scene in the new series where Wycliffe refers to his father's suicide to try and empathize with the son of a missing man.

Nailed to the door in
'Charades'

'The characters of Dixon and Potter will be more defined. Although he hates it, Potter is clearly an office man and this can provide us with the odd moment of humour, which I think is important. Potter is forever coming up with bright – or not-so-bright – ideas and in one instance, it turns out to be he and Dixon who manage to solve the case.

'Not all of the cases in the new series will be murders,' says Kathrine. 'We're not going in for violent armed robberies but we are featuring arson and a missing person. The first series reflected John Burley's books in that there were a lot of crimes of passion. So this time when there are murders, we're tending to avoid crimes of passion.'

Among the cases Wycliffe is called in to solve are: a dangerous Dartmoor prisoner who is helped to escape by a woman prison visitor in order to retrieve his drug profits; a couple who arrive at their holiday home to find the body of a local villain nailed to the kitchen door; the kidnapping of the wife of a stables owner, resulting in a murder investigation among the world of point to point racing; the mystery of two women who both have reason to claim a body washed up on the beach with a shotgun wound to the head as being that of their husband; a schoolgirl found dead in a science lab after a school disco – was it suicide or murder?; and the unsettling effect which the identification of a headless thirty-year-old skeleton has on the landowning Rawle family.

Geraint Morris sums up: 'We hope the combination of a special, clever detective and the magnificent Cornish scenery will again prove irresistible.'

SCENES OF CRIME

It seemed a routine scene. Roger Kitson, walking his dog along the beach in 'The Four Jacks', was shot dead by a mystery sniper. While the body lay on the shoreline, the dog sniffed around anxiously, mourning the loss of his owner.

Since it was a non-speaking role, Kitson was played by a dog handler. So the dog was with its trainer and, more importantly, someone it knew. Thus there was no need to secrete a string of sausages beneath the corpse in order to gain the hound's attention. Everything had been planned down to the last detail. But there was one thing which nobody concerned could cater for – the Cornish weather.

Porthleven, where the opening scenes in 'The Four Jacks' were filmed

That day at Kennack Sands, a force 10 gale howled across the beach, whipping the sea into a frenzy.

'Wycliffe' publicist Jon Day recalls: 'The guy playing Kitson was wearing a wet suit beneath his outer clothes to protect him from the wet beach. But because of the layers of clothing, as he lay there on the beach, it was virtually impossible for him to move. Suddenly this big wave came in and swept him away. The wet suit made him buoyant and there was a real danger that he might have drifted out to sea. Fortunately, the crew were really quick off the mark and rushed over to snatch him from the clutches of the sea before he came to any harm.'

Bearing in mind the old adage about acting with children and animals, it was ironic that the artiste who posed no problems at all that day was the dog. 'The dog was a real star,' says Jon Day. 'It did the whole scene in one take, including lifting its paw on cue.' What a trouper!

Helen Masters remembers the day all too well. 'I had total admiration for that poor guy having to lie on the beach for hours and hours. We were all just being blown sideways and drenched at the same time. At one point we were in this mobile incident room on the beach. The wind was rocking it wildly from side to side until the transport man burst in and said: "Get out now – this thing's going to go!"

'In the end it didn't, but we weren't sorry to get out.

'Another time we were filming on a caravan site and they'd erected some black boards to try and block out the light. But in the strong wind, the boards acted as a sail and the whole thing nearly took off towards the ocean. Summer really didn't begin in Cornwall until two weeks before we finished filming that first series.

'I rented a beautiful little cottage to stay in for the three months we were filming,' adds Helen. 'I had been to Falmouth as a child, when I was about six, but I can't remember much about it. So I was determined to explore Cornwall during any time off. I went for walks along the coast and to the lovely Helford River. When the weather was nice, it was wonderful.'

Jack Shepherd
against a typical
Cornish backdrop

Adam Barker says the conditions in the mobile police unit at Kennack did have a plus side. 'In some ways it was quite fun. We were all in it together and a real community spirit formed to get it done. The fact that we did manage to complete those scenes that day was quite an achievement.'

For Adam, it was an unforgettable introduction to Cornwall. 'I'd never been there before but I soon found out that the weather's not always the way it looks in the brochures – at least not in March and April. With Cornwall, you have to remember that it may look sunny but once you get out on the clifftop, it can be pretty inhospitable. But before Easter last year, we had a lot of wind and rain which made life very difficult.'

Jimmy Yuill says the Cornish weather reminded him of his Scottish roots. 'I even enjoyed the gales we had. It could change every five minutes. You can get all four seasons in one afternoon in Cornwall. It's absolutely magic.'

Jack Shepherd reckons they were just unlucky last year. 'In 1989, I filmed "Ball Trap on the Cote Sauvage" at a Newquay camp site – it doubled up as Brittany – and we had a heatwave in May. It was fantastic for those two weeks.'

He is very fond of Cornwall. 'It's a fascinating landscape and its network of ruined tin mines appealed to the social historian in me. The thing that people forget about Cornwall is that it was the most intensively mined area of the country until 1920. Then the mines ran out and the whole society became bankrupt until the middle classes discovered tourism.'

It didn't take long for Jack to realize the tourism potential of 'Wycliffe'. 'When we were making the pilot, we met a Canadian hiker, aged about sixty-five, and his wife who were travelling from "crime" to "crime" for their summer holidays. It makes you realise the impact of it.'

For Cornish actress Susan Penhaligon, who guest starred in 'The Scapegoat', returning to her home county was a joy. 'Hanging around between takes is usually boring,' she says. 'But I

Beware of crabs! Wycliffe takes a barefoot walk along the beach in 'The Pea Green Boat'

just lay on the cliffs and gawped at the coastline. It's my favourite place in the world. I had a great sense of belonging. I live near the River Thames and when I get homesick, I go and stare morosely at the boats. But somehow it's not the same.'

The first series of 'Wycliffe' was filmed in over a hundred different locations throughout west Cornwall. 'The Four Jacks' took place in Porthleven, Redruth, Portreath, Truro, Carrickowell, Goonhilly, Kennack and Portpean House; 'The Dead Flautist' was filmed at St Newlyn East, St Clement, Godolphin House, Mawgan Church and Trelowarren Mill; 'The Scapegoat' at St Just, Cape Cornwall, Carharrack, St Day, Frontier City near St Columb Major, Pentire and Tregonning; 'The Tangled Web' at Merthen Manor, Mylor, St Dennis, Constantine, Bishops Forum and Treliske Hospital, Truro; 'The Last Rites' at St Ewe, Pentewan, Old Kea and Merther Church; and 'The Pea Green Boat' was filmed at Hayle, Lelant, Godrevy Point, Porkellis, United Downs, Godolphin, Mylor and the cliffs near Porthtowan.

Associate producer Mike Bartley, who has worked on series such as 'The Onedin Line', 'Bergerac', 'Edge of Darkness' and 'Casualty', says: 'We try to show as much of Cornwall as possible

Filming outside Portpean House for 'The Four Jacks'

on screen. People have different expectations of Cornwall. I'm a fishing-village man – St Mawes and Mevagissey – whereas a lot of people like cliffs and thrashing water. We aim to cater for all tastes. Obviously we can't do all of the filming outside – we have to keep some interior locations up our sleeves for weather cover. With a turnaround of just two weeks per episode, we have no time to overrun. But we endeavour to find locations where even the interiors have a good view – like Portpean House, overlooking the sea, that we used on 'The Four Jacks'.

The burning wheel rolls down the hill at Pentire Point for the dramatic opening to 'The Scapegoat'

'It's no secret that we had terrible problems with the weather last year. One of the biggest headaches is that on the coast you get a sea mist which just whites out the screen – you can't see a thing. But our timescale doesn't allow us to pick and choose our weather conditions. If it's pouring with rain or the coast is shrouded in sea mist, we have to film anyway.

'We're based in Truro which is central to Wycliffe's Cornwall, an area that goes east to St Austell and north to Newquay and Wadebridge. We do a lot of filming on National Trust land and are very grateful for their co-operation.'

The man entrusted with finding the perfect spot to film is location manager Roger Elliott. For the past ten years, he has been running his own company, West Country Locations, and has an unparalleled knowledge of where to film in Cornwall. 'Where we film is dictated by the demands of the script,' he says, 'but I'm always on the lookout for locations within an hour's drive of Truro. Despite the hail and snow, wind and rain that we get in late winter and spring, it's better to film then than in the height of summer. Filming in Cornwall in summer would be a nightmare. The traffic on the roads would be so heavy that it would take an eternity travelling to and from locations. Then there are the

Lobster fishermen provided the background for 'The Pea Green Boat'

holidaymakers. It's okay if you want a crowded beach scene but, given that most scenes in "Wycliffe" tend to happen in isolated or near-deserted spots, it just wouldn't work. Basically, if you want a deserted beach scene and are filming in July, forget it!'

Among locations featured in the second series are Perranporth, Cape Cornwall, Newquay, Wadebridge, St. Austell, Truro, Coombe and Redruth.

One of the most demanding tasks on the first series of 'Wycliffe' was finding somewhere to roll a huge burning wheel over a 150-foot cliff and into the sea below for the pagan ceremony in the episode 'The Scapegoat'. It was actually based on a genuine ancient ritual although John Burley borrowed the idea from Brittany rather than Cornwall. The director of that story was Martyn Friend whose television credits include the highly acclaimed 'Love On a Branch Line', 'Inspector Alleyn' and 'Rumpole of the Bailey'.

'We decided that Pentire Point was the ideal spot for throwing the wheel over the cliff,' says Martyn, 'but it was National Trust and we were slightly worried that it was something they wouldn't agree to. Happily, they gave us the go-ahead. The whole shoot was an extremely complicated exercise and one which we were all dreading. We had four wheels with petroleum jelly added to make sure they burned. The wheels were metal, twelve feet in diameter, and extremely heavy. And inside was the effigy of the Scapegoat. We had four cameras on the shot – one taking the wonderful view out towards Pentire Point with the wheel going down the cliff in the middle distance; another almost in the path of the wheel, dug into the hill, the wheel passing within nine inches of it; and two more doing various standard shots.

'Fortune smiled on us that day. It was one of the two days that we had decent weather. And we had to have good weather for it because we had a crowd of sixty villagers playing onlookers. The reason we had four wheels made was to cover ourselves. We couldn't rehearse the scene and we had no idea what sort of path this thing would pursue – how erratic it would be – so we had three spare wheels in case it went wrong. So over a period of a few hours, we rolled these four wheels, one at a time, off the cliff and down into the sea. The extraordinary thing was that it worked beautifully first time, but we still did it three more time because we had no other use for the wheels! So, despite our misgivings beforehand, it turned out to be a wonderful day and good fun. And the villagers really entered into the spirit of it.'

Such are the vagaries of television that although the wheel went into the sea at Pentire, the scenes at the foot of what were supposedly the same cliffs were actually filmed fifty miles away at Cape Cornwall! Again, Martyn Friend got lucky that day.

He recalls: 'We were filming the sequence in "The Scapegoat" where the body was found at the foot of the cliff and the cliff rescue people were going down to investigate when Wycliffe, Kersey and Lane arrived. We were using the local St Just Cliff Rescue Team. They were in their bright yellow suits, we had a real person lying in the surf on the rocks as the body and what with our own crowd and police cars, it obviously looked like the real thing. For the next thing we knew, a helicopter – it was actually an anti-submarine RNAS helicopter – presumably on some sort of operation, came over and had a really good look at us. We thought: "This would be marvellous."

'So one of the crew rushed away and phoned their controller and said: "Look, if you've any helicopters in the area who want to

The helicopter that made the director's day in 'The Scapegoat'

The car that wouldn't go bang - the Jaguar XJS being primed for explosion in 'The Pea Green Boat'

snoop around, snoop around in the background of our shot." They said that if we could wait for twenty minutes, one of their helicopters would come over and spend a bit of time with us. We held fire, did some other shots in the meantime, and ended up with this wonderful shot of the principals at the top of this 150-foot cliff and a huge helicopter hovering in the background with us saying, "Left a bit, right a bit" and so on – all for free. If we'd set it up ourselves, I dread to think what it would have cost but we got it by chance, a bit of initiative and the co-operation of all those concerned.'

Among the most spectacular sequences to date on 'Wycliffe' was the exploding fishing boat at the start of 'The Pea Green Boat'. This was filmed off Godrevy Point near Hayle.

'We bought an old fishing boat, says Nick Middleton, who was responsible for special effects, 'and took out the fuel tank. We replaced it with a portable tank and filmed the shots of the boat going out to sea. Then we removed the engine as well, to comply with anti-pollution laws, and attached charges to the boat. The explosion was done by remote control. It worked really well.'

However another stunt in the same episode, where a red Jaguar XJS plunges off the cliffs and explodes on the beach below, proved more traumatic.

'We filmed that in a cove near Porthtowan,' says Nick. 'We used two identical cars – one for being driven to the edge of the cliff and the other to go over the cliff and for me to put charges in. I had selected a position on the beach to carry out a radio-controlled explosion but they began to fall behind with filming at the top of the cliffs and the tide was coming in. So I had to find a new position to detonate the explosion from the top of the cliffs. When we came to do it, I found that I was out of range and there was no explosion.

'So I had to go down on to the beach. I wouldn't let anyone else near the car in case it suddenly went up. It was pretty nerve-wracking and I approached the car very gingerly. I then had to crawl inside the twisted wreckage to set new charges. Luckily, all went well the second time and the camera managed to catch it on film. All that remained then was for a tractor and trailer to clear all the debris off the beach. But it had been a long day. And I don't mind admitting that when those first charges failed to go off, I could have jumped off the cliff myself!'

The Jaguar plunges over the cliffs near Porthtowan

BODY TALK

'**K**eep calm, don't shake, persevere, keep your eyes closed and whatever you do, don't blink.'

That, according to Lamorna Penrose, is the secret of playing a convincing corpse on television. And she should know. For twenty-year-old Lamorna spent a total of five hours as the body of archaeology student Celia Dawe in the 'Wycliffe' story 'The Four Jacks'. Celia was shot through the head while lying naked in bed and, although she didn't actually die until the end of the episode, she was in a coma throughout and never regained consciousness.

Lamorna Penrose proves there is life after death

'It was really hard work,' remembers Lamorna ruefully. 'It might sound easy just lying there, but believe me it's not. For the scenes on the bed, we were filming in a cottage at Porthleven and it was bitterly cold with the wind howling outside. I was on the bed for about two hours, almost freezing to my own death under just one thin sheet. The close-up shots seemed to take an eternity. For those, I just had to hold my breath and hope. But it's very difficult to keep absolutely still when you're nervous and so cold.'

Worse was to come: Lamorna's next scene meant being lifted up the hill from the cottage in a stretcher by paramedics.

'That took another couple of hours because they kept having to do retakes. And between each take, while everybody else was able to move around and keep warm, I had to remain strapped in the stretcher, because it had taken so long to get me in there in the first place. So I was just deposited on the ground. I didn't enjoy that at all.'

Lamorna's final scene at the hospital was relatively painless and after that she went behind the camera to spend two months as assistant to the property master and art director on 'Wycliffe'.

Lamorna is currently studying costume design in London. 'Playing a corpse has certainly put me off being an actress,' she says. 'Given the choice of playing a corpse and working in costume design, I'd definitely choose the latter!'

THE ACCENT ON CORNWALL

I f there is one thing guaranteed to upset Cornish people, it is hearing an actor failing miserably in an attempt to do a Cornish accent. To prevent that from happening on 'Wycliffe', a dialect coach has been hired to ensure that all of the accents are as authentic as possible.

The dialect coach on the first series was Andrew Jack who has worked on 'The Chief', the 'Indiana Jones' films and has just finished helping actors to perfect Russian accents on the latest Bond movie, 'Goldeneye'.

'People think there is just one Cornish accent,' says Andrew, 'but in fact there are a number of local variations. If you take a word like "butter", you will find that the "t"s are dropped in rural areas. But in really isolated communities, where they might not have television and are thus less influenced by outsiders, the people will tend to say "budder".

'The differences between these local dialects are often very slight and, for us, these local variations are a means of escape. As long as we get the overall accent right, nobody can be too critical of us. For what passes as a Cornish accent in Penzance might be frowned upon down on the Lizard. We just try to get the actors to do a good generic Cornish accent.

'One of the main traits of the Cornish accent is the hard "r". It's the same in the United States – there too, the further west you go, the harder the "r" becomes. And the Cornish "ow" sound is almost French.

'Most actors can do a perfectly capable Cornish accent. They may have to eradicate a slight Midlands accent first, in which case little twangy sounds can give them away. What I do is go along to the readthrough for each episode and listen out for voices and dialects. I will then put my head together with the producer and director and point out which people need some assistance. And then, I'll just sit quietly with whoever needs help and try to eradicate the problem.

'Also after the readthrough, I give the cast a rundown on the Cornish landscape. I tell them about the lie of the land – the wind and the gorse – because I find that helps them understand how the Cornish people speak. If you've lived most of your life in London, it's hard to imagine the allowances you have to make for the wild Cornish elements.'

On the second series of 'Wycliffe', the dialect coach was Alison Mackinnon. She says: 'My main task is to make sure that, where necessary, the guest actors adopt a Cornish accent rather than Mummerset which is the general perception of any accent west of Bristol. The Cornish accent is not burry and dozy, it has subtler textures and is very Celtic. It is clipped rather than warm and round. Most actors have a standard southern accent and it is up to me to help them move away from that.'

Prior to working on 'Wycliffe', Alison was assisting Australian supermodel Elle MacPherson in her bid to acquire a standard English accent for the new Franco Zeffirelli production of 'Jane Eyre'. 'To get Australians to speak in a different accent, you have to get them to find a wider space in their mouth,' says Alison. 'Elle was no problem. She left Australia years ago and so her accent was not that broad. A lot of the corners had been cut off. In fact, I was very impressed with her English accent.'

POLICE PROCEDURE

'Our attention to detail on police procedure is obsessional,' says Jack Shepherd. 'We have a police adviser on set with us while filming to ensure that everything we do is totally authentic.'

The adviser, a serving officer, elaborates: 'I'm there to ensure legal, procedural and attitudinal authenticity. The legal area covers things like the Police and Criminal Evidence Act of 1984 which restricts the number of hours a suspect can be held in custody without being charged. So we can't have the police on TV bringing people in for questioning and then just holding them without any review.

'Procedural relates to the various duties within the force. I might point out that a particular duty would be carried out by an inspector rather than a sergeant and so on. And I help with things like interview technique, the use of equipment, such as handcuffs, plus the correct deployment of the tactical firearms unit as seen in the story "The Four Jacks".

'The question of attitude covers how officers would react to certain situations. Jimmy Yuill might ask me: "Would Kersey say this?" And I will decide whether or not the line is appropriate.

Director Martyn Friend waits to brief the troops

'I also have to make sure that all of the forensic details are correct. John Burley's books are so ingenious that there are people dying of things I've never heard of so I have to check everything out.

'I am involved in the structure of the scripts. At the first draft, I might send back a twenty-page critique with, say, twenty-four points from the script which I think need attention. And I

A scenes of crime officer with the tape used to mark the murder site

carry on like this, the number of criticisms dwindling, until, by the third or fourth version of the script, there are only a few comments from me. That's when the script is ready for filming.

'Of course, I have to be prepared to compromise – I have to remember that, although everyone wants the programme to be credible, it is fiction we are making. And there is little point making criticisms unless I can come up with suitable alternatives. I am not there to be an obstacle to the production process.

'An example was in last year's episode "The Dead Flautist". The scene of a murder is always safeguarded by tapes and, in the case of a building, an officer is stationed at the gate or the door to prevent any unauthorized personnel from going in. But in that episode, there was a scene in which Wycliffe visited the cottage where Miller had recently been killed and found Lord Hugh Bottrell rifling through a desk. I continually challenged that scene, saying that it would never have happened – the area would have been secured properly. The director accepted my point but said that the scene had to stay in for the sake of the story. So we had to reach a compromise with Wycliffe saying to Bottrell: "This is the scene of a murder. Didn't you see the warning tapes?"'

Producer Geraint Morris says: 'The police adviser and I get on very well but I must admit to another mistake we made last year. In the episode "The Last Rites", Kersey, Lane and a couple of other officers were in the pub having a drink at the end of a long day. I know that cops when they are relaxing tend to make a wee bit of noise! Wycliffe was upstairs in his bedroom and he came down and complained, ordering the officers involved in the inquiry to go to bed. That was wrong. In reality, he wouldn't have disturbed his officers. And it just didn't work on screen because Wycliffe is not that kind of leader.

'Our adviser said it would never have happened. He said that if Wycliffe had gone down and told them to go to bed, they'd have given him the two fingers! So our adviser was right and I was wrong. Still, we make sure we learn from any mistakes.'

DRESSED TO KILL

T he man responsible for clothing police and murderers alike on 'Wycliffe' is costume designer Reg Samuel. And he is acutely aware of the need to protect the actors from the ravages of the Cornish weather.

'All of the clothes have to be practical for winter filming,' says Reg. 'We get through a lot of wellies! And for outside filming, the actors invariably have to wear thermals underneath their ordinary clothes.

'I hire the police uniforms from a firm in London but with so many police shows on television, I have to get my order for uniforms in pretty smartly in case supplies run short. I have twenty basic police uniforms in various sizes and we then sew on the stripes for the ranks as required.

'Our main characters are all CID. I take the individual actors shopping but make sure that I have done a recce first so that I can steer them towards the things I want them to have! Since Jack and Helen have stand-in doubles, I have to order two of everything. I tend to get a lot of the clothes from Oxfam shops although sometimes I bring clothes from other productions I work on. For example, after I'd done "The Chief", I brought some clothes with me to be worn by extras on "Wycliffe". But I'm sure nobody will recognize them.'

Reg says the most challenging task to date on 'Wycliffe' has probably been the druids' costumes for 'The Scapegoat'. 'I based the costumes on a Celtic design and it was great fun making those up and doing all the chains and other jewellery. We couldn't make the costumes look too professional, however, since they were supposed to be homemade. But it was nice to be able to do something different like that.'

Costume designer Reg Samuel (right) with another satisfied customer

A CLOSE SHAVE

Make-up designer Sue Bide has no doubt as to the most memorable moment on 'Wycliffe' – it was when a man wandered into her caravan, stark naked. But it was all in the cause of art.

The man was playing the corpse of murdered undertaker Jonathan Riddle in 'The Scapegoat' and was preparing for a scene in which he had to lie naked, face down on rocks at the bottom of a 150-foot cliff.

'He had a nice day for it,' laughs Sue, 'because it was glorious sunshine. He was only on the rocks for about ten minutes and was truly naked – he wasn't wearing a body stocking or anything. Before he did the scene, he had to be made up as if his body had been smashed against the rocks. So he was sitting in my caravan in all his glory while I applied bruises to everywhere except his

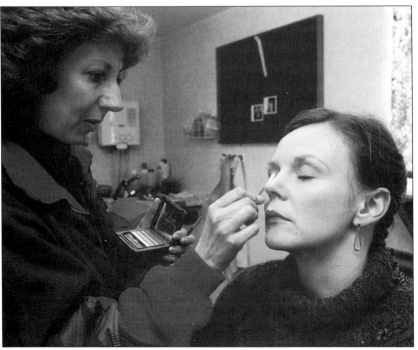

Make-up designer Sue Bide applies the finishing touches

front which couldn't be seen since he was going to lie face down.

'After we had done that, I had to do another scene with the same guy which involved post-mortem stitching. To make sure I got it right, I went beforehand to Treliske Hospital, Truro, and was taken to the mortuary where I was able to see a real corpse who'd had the special post-mortem stitching.

'Unfortunately, the actor in question was really hairy so I had to shave the body hair off his chest before sticking on the special strips to simulate the stitching. Finally, to make it look authentic, I had to stick the hair back on his chest. It was a great deal of effort for both him and me and I must say the finished product looked suitably gruesome. Alas, it was so gruesome that they decided not to show it on TV!

What the well-dressed druid is wearing

'There's not much blood and gore on "Wycliffe" because of the time slot,' says Sue. 'Even when I made up a man who had been blasted to death with a shotgun, it was only seen on screen very briefly.'

All of this is in stark contrast to 'Casualty' on which Sue worked for six years. 'It's just blood, blood and more blood on "Casualty". I'm not squeamish when I do all the blood for television but on "Casualty" we spent an evening in a real hospital casualty department. Seeing real wounds was a different matter altogether. It was quite horrific.'

The contents of Sue's make-up bag is somewhat different to most other women's. 'Apart from my ordinary make-up, I carry around special bruising gels and congealed blood. In fact, I've got a whole kit full of blood and guts. It may sound macabre but I love my job.'

WYCLIFFE'S CORNWALL

'Inland, the Cornish landscape reminds me of my native Yorkshire. And it has the most spectacular coastline you could ever wish to see.' – JACK SHEPHERD

U ntil 1859 when the railway reached the far west and crossed the River Tamar into Cornwall via Brunel's magnificent Saltash bridge, Cornwall had been virtually cut off from the rest of England. For centuries the Tamar, twisting in a narrow valley, then widening into a tidal estuary, had kept Cornwall in splendid isolation. There was not a bridge below the narrow medieval New Bridge at Gunnislake miles up from the sea. As a result, Cornwall retained its own identity – its tiny, almost secretive, fishing ports, its Celtic sentiments and its dialect which, although English, is littered with words surviving from the old Cornish language. Thus it is scarcely surprising that many Cornishmen still see the county as being separate from the remainder of the country. Cornish independence is still alive and kicking.

Wycliffe's Cornwall is the far west of the county stretching down to Land's End (and beyond to the Isles of Scilly), its eastern borders being Newquay to the north and St Austell to the south. It is an area of stark contrasts – from the storm-whipped cliffs at Kennack and the untamed beauty of Cape Cornwall to the picture-postcard fishing villages of Mousehole and Mevagissey and the golden sands of Marazion and St Ives. Although best known for its spectacular coastline, Cornwall also boasts a unique interior landscape where ruined tin mines sit alongside remote farmhouses and green valleys and hills crowd together, the perfect contrast to the rugged rocks of the coast.

English Channel and St George's Channel. Offshore lie The Brisons, a notoriously dangerous rock formation, reputed to have once been used as a sinister open-air prison.

Beyond Whitesand Bay and Sennen Cove is Land's End, home to some of the most magnificent cliff scenery in Britain. Longships Lighthouse lies due west of the last group of rocks while some eight miles further out to sea is Wolf Rock. Just over a mile south-east of Land's End in Nanjizal Bay, archways of orange lichen-encrusted granite rise from a dazzling ultramarine sea. It is a spectacular sight.

Twenty-eight miles from Land's End are the Isles of Scilly, the veritable outpost of Wycliffe's Cornwall. The Scillies consist of over 300 islands but only five are inhabited. The boat from Penzance docks at Hugh

Cod moves in mysterious ways

Town, the small capital of the largest island, St Mary's. Above Hugh Town stands the Elizabethan fort of Star Castle which was converted into a hotel in 1933. The dungeons are now a bar. The other inhabited islands are St Martin's, Tresco (notable for the sub-tropical gardens of Tresco Abbey and the seventeenth-century Cromwell's Castle), Bryher and St Agnes.

Back on the mainland, the coast winds east from Land's End towards Penzance. Set on the cliffside overlooking the beach at Porthcurno Bay is the Minack Open-Air Theatre, a Greek-style amphitheatre where professional companies perform during the summer months. The Minack was created in 1932 by Rowena Cade for a performance of *The Tempest*. Stone seats have since replaced the original grassy ledges but the sight of the moon rising over the backcloth of ocean remains a memorable experience. The eastern arm of Porthcurno Bay is provided by Treryn Dinas which boasts a thirty-six-acre Iron Age cliff fort with a complex of defensive ditches. Nearby is the famous Logan Rock,

Filming on the beach for 'The Pea Green Boat'

a sixty-six-ton monster which was once able to be rocked by hand. But then in the nineteenth century, Hugh Goldsmith, the nephew of poet Oliver Goldsmith, enlisted the help of a gang of sailors and decided to move it for a prank. Such was the outrage that he was obliged to replace it at his own expense. This he somehow managed but the fine balance of the rocking stone was lost.

A few miles east of Logan Rock is tranquil Lamorna Cove, reached by a fertile valley, complete with bubbling trout stream. The artist Samuel John Birch was so enchanted by the place that he changed his name to S.J. Lamorna Birch. At the top of the valley is Boleigh, site of the last battle between the Cornish and the English, in 935. Nearby are The Merry Maidens, a Bronze Age circle of nineteen stones, reputed to be a group of young girls turned to granite for dancing on the Sabbath. On the other side of the road stand two more large standing stones known as The Pipers. Legend has it that these were the musicians who accompanied the dancers and met with the same fate.

Mousehole (pronounced Mouzel) is the prettiest of Cornish fishing villages with narrow lanes and passageways flanked by neat granite cottages encircling a splendid little harbour. In 1595, the village was raided by Spanish privateers and razed to the ground. The only building to survive was the manor house which later became the Keigwin Arms and is now a private residence. A more recent tragedy occurred on the night of 19 December 1981 when the eight-man crew of the local lifeboat was lost in mountainous seas gallantly trying to rescue the crew of the coaster *Union Star* which had been pounded on to the cliffs west of Lamorna. On 23 December each year, Tom Bawcock's Eve recalls the time a local fisherman saved the village from famine by sailing out in a raging storm and returning with a sizeable catch featuring seven different species of fish. A special dish, starry-gazy pie, with fish heads poking up through the pastry, is still baked and eaten in his honour.

Newlyn is the busiest fishing port in the south-west and, like St Ives ten miles away on the other side of the Penwith peninsula, has established a lively artists' colony. The Newlyn School of Painting was founded by Irish artist Stanhope Forbes who came to the town for a few days in 1884 and stayed on. High above the bay is Mount Misery where anxious wives and sweethearts would watch during storms, fearful that their fishermen husbands might not return.

Along the seafront stands the lively town of Penzance. The arrival of the railway in 1859 greatly improved access and its sheltered position at the western end of Mount's Bay made Penzance a fashionable Victorian watering place. Large hotels sprang up and the town boasts handsome Georgian, Regency and Victorian buildings, terraces and squares. One of the most remarkable buildings is the Georgian Egyptian House with its flamboyant facade. On the other side of Chapel Street is the Union

Hotel. It was from a minstrel's gallery in the hotel's Assembly Room that news of Nelson's victory and death at Trafalgar was first announced. Elizabeth Branwell, mother of the Bronte sisters, lived at 25 Chapel Street. Penzance's most famous son is Sir Humphrey Davy, inventor of the miners' safety lamp. His statue stands in front of the Market Hall.

From Penzance, the road follows the vast, magnificent sweep of Mount's Bay to the old smugglers' port of Marazion which combines golden sands with a spectacular view of St Michael's Mount. Marazion is connected to St Michael's Mount by a cobbled causeway, negotiable at low tide. St Michael's Mount has been a place of pilgrimage since the Middle Ages. It is thought that it was once a landlocked hill surrounded by marshy woodland until the sea encroached. The story goes that in 495 the archangel St Michael appeared to a group of fishermen on a large rock (subsequently christened St Michael's Chair), thus establishing its position as a place of worship. In 1135, a Benedictine priory was established on the Mount. The monks' domestic buildings are now incorporated in the fourteenth-century castle on the summit. St Michael's Mount is steeped in history. In 1497, Perkin Warbeck left his wife on the Mount to make an abortive claim for the throne of England; in 1549, the owners of the castle were involved in the Prayer Book Rebellion; and in 1642, at the height of the Civil War, the future Charles II was given sanctuary there en route for the Isles of Scilly.

The principal town on the Lizard Peninsula is Helston, famous since the seventeenth century for Flora Day held on 8 May to welcome spring. The town was once a bustling port but during the thirteenth century a bank of shingle formed at the mouth of the Loe River, barring access to the sea. Loe Pool, the freshwater lake that built up behind the barrier, is Cornwall's largest lake. It is one of two sites in Cornwall (the other is Dozmary Pool on Bodmin Moor) where King Arthur's sword, Excalibur, was said to have been grasped by a hand rising up from the water. A thatched cottage in Wendron Street, Helston, was the birthplace of 'Battling' Bob Fitzsimmons, England's first world heavyweight boxing champion. Nearby Porthleven was the birthplace of Dambusters' hero Guy Gibson.

East of Helston, at the head of the beautiful Helford River, lies Gweek, a peaceful little village now home to the Cornish Seal Sanctuary. A narrow, winding lane leads to the pretty village of Mawgan, set in a wooded valley, and on to Frenchman's Creek, immortalized by Daphne du Maurier's book of the same name. The Lizard Downs to the south are quite dominated by the huge communication dishes of British Telecom's satellite earth station at Goonhilly and at Poldhu Cove on the west coast is a memorial to wireless pioneer Guglielmo Marconi. It was on these high cliffs overlooking Mount's Bay that in 1900 Marconi decided to erect a vast wireless station. On 12

Wycliffe on the rocks?

December 1901, signals sent from Poldhu were received by Marconi on the other side of the Atlantic at St John, Newfoundland, marking the birth of wireless telegraphy. Other villages on the Lizard – such as Mullion, Gunwalloe, Coverack and Cadgwith – have remained gloriously untouched by twentieth-century technology. But the peace and tranquility on a summer afternoon hide a grim reminder of the dangers of the coastline when conditions are less pleasant. The church tower at St Keverne on the east coast of the Lizard Peninsula acts as a daymark to sailors, helping them to avoid a notorious group of rocks called the Manacles on the approach to Helford and Falmouth Bay. In the churchyard are the tombstones of over 400

Wycliffe at the wall of
a Cornish harbour

men who have perished along this stretch of coast. Lizard Point
itself is the most southerly point on the British mainland and it
was from these cliffs that the Spanish Armada was first sighted in
1588. The first lighthouse on The Lizard was established in 1619,
using open coal fires. It was the brainchild of Sir John Killigrew of
Falmouth but shipowners refused to pay fees to support the
venture and even accused Killigrew of averting potential wrecks
on The Lizard so that they might instead be wrecked within his
own territory further up the coast where he held rights of salvage.
A regular light was not established until 1752 and today's can be

seen at a distance of sixty-four miles on a clear night.

With a position at the entrance to a large stretch of deep, sheltered water – the estuary of no fewer than seven rivers – Falmouth was once Britain's second busiest port. Prior to the sixteenth century, it was nothing more than a small fishing village known as Penny-come-quick, but first Henry VIII, then Sir Walter Raleigh and the Killigrew family brought about a rapid expansion. Pendennis Castle and its smaller neighbour across the water, St Mawes, were built by Henry on either side of the entrance to Carrick Roads to defend the new port against possible French invaders. For 200 years, Falmouth was the base for the 'Packet Service' sailing ships but the introduction of steam saw their decline. And by 1850, Southampton had taken over as the Packet port. Down the centuries, Falmouth has received many famous visitors (often at the end of epic voyages) and Kenneth Grahame began *The Wind in the Willows* at the town's Green Bank Hotel.

As Falmouth increased in prosperity, so the neighbouring port of Penryn, situated further up the Penryn River, declined. Penryn had earlier been hit by the closure, in 1549, of Glasney collegiate church which, for the previous 300 years, had been a centre for religious instruction renowned throughout Europe. Across the river is the village of Flushing. It was originally called Nankersey but when Dutch engineers arrived to build Falmouth's quays, they settled there and changed the name as a reminder of their home country. The cottages cling to the waterside and Flushing is reputed to have the mildest climate in Britain.

The focal point of Truro is the cathedral. Completed in 1910, it was the first cathedral to be built in Britain since St Paul's. Once a major port in conjunction with Falmouth, Truro's shipping declined with the silting up of the higher reaches of the Truro River. For a while the town went into the doldrums but enjoyed a dramatic revival in the early nineteenth century as an elegant Georgian town christened the 'London of the West'. Lemon Street, rising steeply to the south of the city, is considered one of the best-preserved complete Georgian streets in England. Truro is also renowned for its narrow alleyways or 'opes' with evocative names like Squeezegutts Alley.

Truro is surrounded by beautiful villages, among them Probus (with Cornwall's highest church tower at 123 feet 6 inches) and St Clement (resplendent with thatched cottages). At Tresillian in 1646, the Civil War ended when the Royalist Lord Hopton surrendered to the Parliamentary forces under Fairfax. The Parliamentarians had their headquarters at the Wheel Inn. Trelissick Gardens, with superb views over the River Fal, is a delightful National Trust property with rare shrubs and plants and a four-mile woodland nature trail. At nearby Come-to-Good stands a thatched Quaker meeting house, built in 1710. Its name stems from the Cornish for 'House in the wooded combe'. Across the King Harry Ferry (named after Henry VI) from Trelissick is Tolverne, a tiny village which served as a departure point for Second World War troop carriers. Earlier, it had been a contraband centre and there is still a thatched smugglers' cottage at the water's edge.

To the south-east of Truro, on the opposite bank of the Carrick Roads from Falmouth, is the Roseland Peninsula, a small paradise with woodlands and sheltered creeks to the north and rocky cliff on the coast. Running down its centre is the winding Percuil River. The thirteenth-century church at St Just-in-Roseland, with its creekside setting of tropical trees, is arguably the most picturesque in the whole of Britain. From Gerrans village, a four-mile walk along the coastpath to St Anthony Head and its lighthouse offers superb panoramic views on all sides. The church of St Anthony at Place is steeped in legend. It is said to have once been a Celtic monastery, the history of which is written between the two rows of dog teeth on the south door. The story goes that Christ visited this peninsula when his uncle, Joseph of Arimathea, came to trade for tin. When they were off St Anthony Head, a storm blew up and they sheltered in the little bay below Place Manor. While making the ship seaworthy again, they camped there, leaving a shrine behind them and some years later, the church was built on that site. At the mouth of the Percuil River stands St Mawes, a popular yachting venue. Its steep lanes contain a number of charming old cottages whose gardens overflow with flowers.

Beyond the small fishing village of Portscatho, Gerrans Bay and Nare Head lies Veryan Bay. The village of Veryan is located a few miles inland and is best known for its whitewalled circular nineteenth-century round houses, each topped with a conical thatched roof and a cross and situated at either end of the village. Some say that a local vicar built them to keep the devil out and away from his daughters, the belief being that the devil likes to hide and lie in wait in corners. A lane runs from the village down a lovely wooded valley to sandy Pendower Beach with its disused lime kiln. Travelling north-east from Veryan, the road descends the high cliffs to the coves at Portholland and Porthluney. Visible from the beach are the turrets of Caerhays Castle, a fairytale mansion built by John Nash in 1808.

On the other side of Dodman Point ('the noblest of Cornish headlands' and featured in Sir Arthur Quiller-Couch's book *Dead Man's Rock*) is Gorran Haven, a small port which sustained a strong fishing rivalry with Mevagissey in the halcyon days of the pilchard. South of Mevagissey is Portmellon, a noted ship-building village. Percy Mitchell started his shipyard there in 1924 and went on to construct a vast variety of vessels, ranging from seven-foot dinghies to ships of over thirty tons. Mevagissey itself is one of Cornwall's quaintest fishing villages, much loved by tourists who crowd around the compact harbour in the height of summer. Pilchards were once the mainstay of the economy, thousands of tons a year being caught, cured and exported to Italy or sold to the Royal Navy whose seamen called them 'Mevagissey Ducks'. As well as providing food, pilchards also yielded oil which was used in domestic lamps for light and warmth. An old fishermen's rhyme goes: 'Food, heat and light. All in one night.'

Inland, Grampound was a bustling port during Norman times when the sea carried ships there. Its steep main street still boasts some interesting buildings including a toll-house by the bridge (once the lowest bridging point on the River Fal) and a tannery where traditional bark-tanning methods are still employed, the only one of its kind remaining in Cornwall.

The most easterly point of Wycliffe's Cornwall is the town of St Austell, the capital of the china clay industry. It was in 1755 that William Cookworthy first discovered sizeable deposits of china clay or kaolin in Cornwall. Originally used for making porcelain, it is now used for coating paper and in the manufacture of household paints and some medicines. Britain went on to become the world's leading exporter of china clay, and to the north of St Austell can be seen a series of white 'mountains', waste heaps from the industry. These are known locally, but not always affectionately, as the Cornish Alps!

A more natural series of uplands can be found to the south-west of Wadebridge. These are the St Breock Downs, the centrepiece of which is the St Breock Standing Stone, a prehistoric monument once some sixteen feet high.

The attractive town of Wadebridge is home to the longest bridge in Cornwall – the fourteen-arch structure which crosses the River Camel. It is known as 'The Bridge on Wool', thought to mean that its fifteenth-century foundations were laid on packs of wet, compressed wool to reinforce the sandy soil. Another explanation suggests that the money raised to pay for the bridge came principally from wealthy sheep farmers, eager for an easier passage across the river. The Royal Cornwall Show is held at Wadebridge in June.

Between Wadebridge and Newquay, at the head of the Vale of Lanherne, is the little market town of St Columb Major. It was considered as a possible site for Cornwall's cathedral but lost out to the more centrally placed Truro. The town is best known for the Shrove Tuesday hurling contest when a ball of silver-coated applewood is used in the Town versus Country game. The object of the exercise is to carry the ball to one of two goals, situated two miles apart at either end of the town. The resultant battle is often fierce with a total disregard for any rules.

From St Columb, the road sweeps down to Newquay with a fine outlook over Newquay Bay. In Wycliffe's Cornwall, you're never far from a breathtaking view.

JACK SHEPHERD
AS DETECTIVE SUPERINTENDENT CHARLES WYCLIFFE

J ack Shepherd's first visit to Cornwall was very nearly his last. For back in the 1950s, he almost drowned while on a family holiday at Praa Sands, a popular mile-long stretch of beach on Mount's Bay between Penzance and Porthleven.

'I was born in Leeds and the family tradition was to go to Whitby for our annual holiday. Then in the early Fifties, when I was eleven or twelve, my parents decided it would be good to broaden our horizons and go to other parts of the country, and so

Wycliffe picks his way through the clues

we went to Penzance one year. But my principal memory of the holiday was nearly getting drowned at Praa Sands when I got into difficulties in the sea. The waves were a little rougher than I had anticipated and I had to be pulled to safety. It was a nasty experience.

'The other thing I remember was being keen on photography at the time and dragging my parents off to Carn Euny, an Iron Age village between Penzance and Land's End. We went on to Land's End afterwards but missed the last bus and had to walk all the way back to Penzance.'

Jack Shepherd *is* Wycliffe. In interviews, he answers questions politely, thoughtfully and methodically as if weighing up the evidence. Like Wycliffe, he has a quiet air of authority, both men having risen through the ranks of their chosen professions to a position where they command enormous respect from their peers. As befits an actor of his standing, his approach to playing Wycliffe was thorough and considered.

'At the start of "Wycliffe", I asked John Burley what sort of copper Wycliffe was and he said that he was the sort of copper he'd have been if he had been a cop. That set me off thinking, 'Well in that case, that's what I'd better do too." So I began imagining the kind of policeman I'd have been if I had become a policeman instead of going to university and also trying to envisage what the case would do to me, how it would affect me.

'It was an interesting exercise because back in 1970, when I was twenty-nine, I appeared in "Budgie" as perhaps the least convincing policeman ever seen on television. He was a comic character called Detective Constable Leadbetter and he was as big a loser as a policeman as Budgie was as a crook. And that was the kind of policeman I'd have been then. It was unthinkable that someone like I was in those days could have become a policeman – not because of any hippy principles but because I was temperamentally unsuitable. I was the opposite of everything you could imagine a policeman to be. But I think I could do the job now. And that's simply the result of another twenty years of living. It changes your outlook on life.

'I'm a different person now – I am good at finding things out about people. So I feel at home as Wycliffe. He has a lot of my psychological attitudes. He doesn't suffer fools gladly and if he thinks people are crooked, he is very tough.'

There was a police presence in Jack's family however. 'My late uncle Fred – my dad's brother – was an Inspector with the Metropolitan Police until he retired in the 1960s. He lived in Battersea and we often used to visit him. The thing I remember about him was when I was about eleven, I tried to give some money to a guy on the Embankment who was playing the violin. I felt very sorry for this poor old man and ran up to him to give him a small amount of change but uncle Fred literally took the money out of the man's hands and said: "Don't be stupid, lad. He earns more than your father." And that's given me a problem dealing with beggars ever since. It's coloured my attitude towards them.'

Playing Wycliffe has presented Jack with a considerable challenge. 'I read the books and had a pretty good idea how to pitch Wycliffe but I don't think I really got under his skin until I met John Burley. To my mind, Wycliffe is based on John. John should have been a detective himself.

'Very little is known about Wycliffe the person. There's hardly anything about his background in the books apart from the fact that he's from Liverpool. But we decided that he ought to come from Yorkshire since I do. He's married with two children but after the pilot, "Wycliffe and the Cycle of Death", the ITV schedulers said there should be no scenes with his family. That doesn't stop us talking about them but it has to be done via phone calls.

'So in the pilot, I was discovering the character as I went along. Then last year, before we came to do series one, I asked our police adviser the question which for my money is the key question to anyone playing a policeman. And that was: "Are you two separate individuals?" Is there a professional copper which is a persona – a thing you wear first thing in the morning to protect you from the gruesome nature of the job and when you get home, you take that off like a coat and revert to the normal person you'd hope to be?

'That's an interesting acting challenge but our adviser said that in his opinion, that isn't true. You're the same person all day long. He said when a policeman first starts out, there probably are two characters as you learn how to cope with the job, but by the time you've reached the age that Wycliffe is now – his early fifties – you've sorted that out.

'Wycliffe is very much a professional policeman who is much more dangerous and

Talking to author John Burley was a vital part of Jack Shepherd's investigation into the character of Wycliffe

certainly tougher than I first imagined. I liken him to a crocodile swimming just beneath the surface waiting to pounce. The moment a suspect makes a mistake, out come the teeth and he snaps into action. He has a good brain – he's intelligent, thoughtful, quiet, a methodical thinker. One of the areas we've investigated in the second series is the idea of him being a master interrogator. Not only has he got a wonderful intuition about who did things and he's very deductive, but he's also a brilliant interrogator. That involves him becoming the kind of person whom he thinks the person he's interrogating will relate to. He will adapt as to whether he's talking to, say, a woman or a tough guy. He will ingratiate himself or bully slightly depending on the circumstances. So he's rather like an actor really. He's playing around with his personality to get results. And I find that fascinating.

Wycliffe uses his initiative to bring the murderous activities of Sid Passmore to an end in 'The Scapegoat'

'One of the few clues about Wycliffe's personality to emerge from the first series came in "The Tangled Web". He was planning to spend a weekend away with his wife and had loaded up his car boot accordingly. Then an old woman's body was discovered in a freezer and he had to work instead. But we saw him putting his suitcase into the boot. There was a saxophone magazine, a fishing line and some golf clubs. There were a lot of clues in five seconds as the boot went up. I would certainly like him to be interested in jazz because I am. And Penzance is full of jazz clubs.

'Unlike "NYPD Blue", which is my favourite American police series, "Wycliffe" is not character-based. It is very much a whodunit, even a whydunit. For example in the pilot, although Wycliffe was clear who had done it, no one was arrested because there was insufficient evidence. I suppose I see the series as being half-way between something like "Softly, Softly", which was about police procedure, and "Inspector Morse" which was about a fantasy copper who, through his genius, solved extremely difficult crimes. The Wycliffe books are whodunits but I feel that our series is pitched between those two areas.

'"Wycliffe" is not about criminals,' continues Jack. 'It's not cops and robbers. It's about ordinary people – working-class, middle-class, aristocracy – who, because of certain pressures, have broken the law and somebody has usually ended up being killed. They are crimes that could happen in any house in any street. But as you look closer, you find all kinds of incredible events and secret lives. Wycliffe uncovers the most horrific secrets – affairs, clandestine sexuality, pornography, hatreds at a very ordinary level. Because there's none of Wycliffe's private life, he is very much a medium in allowing these stories to come through. I suspect that's part of the reason why the series is successful – it's the ordinary nature of the people involved. Viewers think 'There but for the grace of God go I."

'I'm an armchair detective myself and love the thoughtful type of thrillers by writers like Dorothy L. Sayers. In those novels, you have the chance to work out whodunit for yourself as the story unfolds. I rather hope we've captured some of that style with "Wycliffe".'

The son of a cabinet maker, Jack Shepherd made his film debut in 'The Virgin Soldiers' in 1969 but it was in 1976 that he shot to fame as Trevor Griffiths' rebellious left-wing MP, Bill Brand, in the series of the same name. It not only brought him widespread acclaim but the undesirable side-effect of being a marked man in pubs.

'People used to come up to me in pubs and hit me when I was Bill Brand. They'd say: "So you think you're a tough guy?" And then it was whack!

'At that time, I had no interest whatsoever in being in a series. I did Bill Brand for twelve episodes and that was enough. I wanted to do different things. The shelf life of a series actor isn't very

Wycliffe questions
Mrs Tremaine (Anne
Stallybrass) in 'The Pea
Green Boat'

long, just a few months really. People remember you for those few months, then the memory fades and they think they've seen you at their sister's wedding.'

Jack chose his parts carefully over the next few years, among them 'Ready When You Are, Mr McGill', 'Ten Days That Shook the Branch', 'Count Dracula', 'Mr and Mrs Bureaucrat', 'Sons and Lovers' and 'Bulman'. He also developed his talents as a writer, contributing 'Underdog' and 'Clapperclaw' for television. Much of his time was spent in the theatre and in 1983 he won the Theatre Actor of the Year Award for *Glengarry Glen Ross*.

He has steadfastly refused to compromise his principles by appearing in commercials. 'It doesn't seem worth it to me to do a job that doesn't mean anything – to do it just for the money. I was nearly in one for porridge, directed by Alan Parker, but I refused to cut my hair for it, and Dick Lester asked me to play Richard III for a Cadbury's advert. I thought seriously about that but said no. I had a young family then and could have done with the money, but I thought the money should have gone to someone who was desperate for it.'

After eight years at the National Theatre, Jack started looking around at television again in 1986. 'People had forgotten I existed. I didn't get employed. I had to swallow my pride and start at the bottom again but in my first year back on television, I was only fully employed for six weeks. It wasn't enough.'

Steadily, the roles began to come in – 'Escape From Sobibor', 'A Day in Summer', 'The Murderers Are Among Us', 'Ball-Trap on the Côte Sauvage', a tough cop in 'Between the Lines' and a memorable portrayal of John Stalker, the former Deputy Chief Constable of Manchester, in 'Shoot to Kill'.

Then came the offer to do 'Wycliffe'. 'It was Pennant Roberts, the director of the pilot, who saw me as Wycliffe and I was flattered to be asked. As an actor, there's nothing worse than having nothing to do so when it came up, I saw it as a regular income and continuous employment. It seems that ITV in particular are making more and more detective shows and less and less of anything else. If you want to be employed, you don't have a great deal of choice but to do detectives. I was worried that perhaps there were too many detective series on TV but then again the reason there are so many is because they sell all over the world.

'"Wycliffe" was a gamble on my part. Three years ago, I was offered a three-year contract with HTV. There was no script, just a book, *The Cycle of Death*. They said: "Do you want to do this pilot and if it's successful, you'll be commissioned to do two years of series?"

'I gambled and said yes. I thought it was interesting enough to have a go at. One of the main attractions was just working a lot, being in something where the pressure was enormous, being filmed day after day and really getting your teeth into it.'

It was almost a costly gamble since Jack was badly shaken up in a car crash on the last week of filming the first series. He and guest star Brigit Forsyth were being taken by taxi to the set when a car suddenly pulled out in front of them. The taxi struck it head on.

Jack recalls: 'If I hadn't been wearing a seat belt, I wouldn't be alive now. I was thrown against the seat belt so my rib cage took the impact. Brigit thought I was dying because of the noise I was making, but I was only winded.'

Wycliffe in thoughtful mood

He was taken to hospital for X-rays. 'I was in so much pain, they thought I had broken a rib, but I hadn't. They gave me a jar full of painkillers and sent me on my way. I also cracked a bone in my hand but it was the excruciating pain in my chest that knocked me back a lot.'

'The odd thing,' adds Jack, 'was that our crash was mirrored identically in the first scene we shot next day for the episode "The Pea Green Boat". It took place outside a garage on a main road – just as ours had. I was supposed to be in that crash too, but a stunt man stood in for me.'

Jack has five children – daughter Jan and son Jake from his first marriage and nineteen-year-old twins Victoria and Catherine and son Ben, eighteen, from his second marriage to TV producer Ann Scott. As well as playing the saxophone, he enjoys reading history books in his rambling Victorian house in Dulwich, south London. Fame still holds little interest for him. 'The punters know the face and that's fine by me. I was never one to worry about being a personality. I don't mind being pigeonholed now. In my twenties, I played a lot of teachers, then lawyers, then MPs and now it's policemen.

'For the time being, I am happy doing "Wycliffe". It began as an orphan and I've enjoyed the creative side of it. It's fair to say that the pilot book wasn't the ideal book of John Burley's to adapt. But we beefed the first series up with more action and car chases and this year we've done fresh scripts which is much easier for the writers. Also they've had more time than they had last year.

'I'm learning about "Wycliffe" all the time, and that I enjoy. The programme is still in the process of creating itself. As long as that creative process continues, I'll be interested in it. When that stops, I stop.'

JIMMY YUILL
AS DETECTIVE INSPECTOR DOUG KERSEY

Jimmy Yuill is delighted with the public reaction to no-nonsense west-country copper Doug Kersey.

'People really seem to have taken to him,' says Jimmy. 'I've already had letters from women saying they want to cuddle him. I think they like him because he seems to be a bit of a loner but at the same time strong and honest. It's certainly a novelty for me. I never get to play sexy roles – not that I would consider for a moment that Kersey falls into that category.

'In fact, he's never really had any luck with women at all. When he chatted up a WPC and she finally agreed to go out with him, he suddenly panicked. He was expecting to be rebuffed again. It's almost as if he's programmed for rejection.

'Kersey is very much a man of the earth, a local guy who is trusted by the Cornish people. And that makes him invaluable to Wycliffe who, coming from Yorkshire, is sometimes treated as an outsider. But because he had a spell in the army, serving in the Falklands, Kersey hasn't spent all his life in the south-west and so doesn't have an insular attitude. He can see things from both sides.

'You can tell he's a country man rather than a townie because he's the only one who can stand the cold – he doesn't need to wear a top coat all the time.

'It is his experience in the Falklands which has left him wary of showing emotion although he did express his very real concerns when it was rumoured that Wycliffe might be transferred. For Wycliffe is Kersey's commanding officer and Kersey is someone who needs a commanding

Jimmy Yuill as Doug Kersey

officer. He can lead but is happier taking orders. He knows his place.

'Kersey tends to see things in black and white and act on instinct with the result that he sometimes speaks before he thinks,' says Jimmy who does all his own stunts, including a scene which involved him diving for cover during an explosion. 'Kersey is a very physical character but his aggression is channelled. I wouldn't like to get on his wrong side however!'

When he learned he had got the part, Jimmy deliberately refrained from reading John Burley's Wycliffe books. 'I wanted to play Kersey from the scripts rather than the books because it's through the scripts that the character has to develop, not the books. Also, the character of Kersey on TV is slightly different from John Burley's original creation. In the books, Kersey often gets things wrong but I didn't want to portray him as another bumbling policeman – I wanted to get away from all that. Apart from anything else, I thought if he was that incompetent, why would Wycliffe, who is nobody's fool, want him on his team?

'I think the closeness of Wycliffe, Kersey and Lane has great possibilities. They are so different. Kersey and Lane, in particular, are like chalk and cheese. Kersey may be viewed as old-fashioned, but far from it. He actually quite likes the idea of a woman on the force.'

Jimmy was born in Sutherland, in the far north of Scotland, yet sees many similarities with Cornwall at the opposite end of mainland Britain. 'The accents are similar and so are the people and the music. The landscapes have a lot in common too. Cornwall has two coasts and Sutherland three and both have inland moors, although Sutherland also has mountains. Cornish people tend to speak quickly to combat the frequent gales they get down there. Otherwise their words get lost on the wind. So there is an interesting contrast with the more urban Lane who speaks slower. For Kersey, I adopted a very gentle, generic Devon and Cornwall accent. I couldn't be too precise simply because I've heard so many different local dialects.'

Appearing in school plays in his native Highlands had given

Jimmy an early interest in acting but his burning desire was to be a vet – coincidentally an ambition he shared with Helen Masters who plays Lane in 'Wycliffe'. However the thought of seven years of studying to qualify as a vet eventually put him off the idea and, after a teaching stint in the Falklands in 1975, he went to drama school in London with the intention of pursuing an acting career.

'I hated the whole regime of drama school,' says Jimmy, 'and only stuck it for eight weeks. It so happened that one of the lecturers was leaving at the same time and he told me that if I really wanted to act, he could fix me up with an Equity card and get me a part in a play, *The Jesuit*, at the Traverse Theatre. Because I knew no better, I thought it must always be that easy to get an Equity card. Now, of course, I know different. I played a soldier, Will, in *The Jesuit* and although I was thrown in at the deep end, the play was really good to me and we went on to do it on radio.'

Jimmy's career has since gone from strength to strength. As a member of the Royal Shakespeare Company, he appeared in *A Midsummer Night's Dream* and *Hamlet* and toured the United States with *Nicholas Nickleby*. He has also worked extensively with Kenneth Branagh's Renaissance Company – including films such as 'Henry V', 'Much Ado About Nothing' and 'Frankenstein' and stage productions of *King Lear* and *Coriolanus*.

'In all, I've appeared in about a dozen of Ken's productions.

Jimmy Yuill relaxes with the crew during a break in filming

Kersey listens to
Dixon's words of
wisdom

He's really good to work with. I can't understand why some people choose to knock him. Recently, I've been writing the music for his latest film, "In the Bleak Midwinter". I couldn't appear in that because of my commitments with "Wycliffe". I'm not a professional musician but I find that as an actor, I can interpret a script musically. So I always get the script and then provide the music for it. Even then, it's only something I do as a sideline and usually just for friends.'

On television, Jimmy's appearances have included 'Boon', 'A Square Mile of Murder', 'Inspector Alleyn', 'The Omega Factor', 'Demob' and 'Murder at the Farm'.

'For some reason, I am often cast as a policeman although I can't imagine anyone who feels less like a cop than me. I was in "The Interrogation of John" with Denis Quilley, I played an anti-terrorist policeman in an episode of "The Bill" and back in 1983, I was in "Killer", the first ever "Taggart" story. I was the third policeman behind Taggart and Livingstone but I didn't think the series had any future!'

While filming the latest series of 'Wycliffe', Jimmy switched to the other side of the law to play a rogue in the new BBC detective series 'Hamish Macbeth'.

'I went straight from filming the first series of "Wycliffe" in Cornwall up to the Scottish Highlands to film "Hamish Macbeth". Yet for all these Celtic associations, I live with my wife and two young children in Suffolk. The irony is that since we moved there in 1986, I have only ever had three days' work in East Anglia. I seem to spend the rest of my time travelling all over the place. Still, you can't have everything …'

HELEN MASTERS
AS DETECTIVE INSPECTOR
LUCY LANE

Helen Masters became convinced that she was never going to land the part of Wycliffe's glamorous sidekick Lucy Lane. For the problem of finding the right actress to play Lane seemed to take longer to solve than one of Wycliffe's murder cases.

'HTV's casting director Sarah Bird had had me in for one or two other things in the past,' remembers Helen, 'and then she came to see me in a play I was doing on the London fringe called *Acid Hearts*. After that, I was called in to meet Ferdy Fairfax who was directing the first "Wycliffe". He told me I was completely wrong for the part. He envisaged a short girl with spiky hair whereas I am quite tall and at the time had long, flowing hair.

'Nevertheless, we get on very well and I was recalled three times. The more often you're recalled, the closer it means you are to getting the part which also means that each recall gets more horrific. Each time you become more nervous – the whole thing gets more and more traumatic.

'Then I heard that it was down to just the two of us. But the problem in that situation is you don't know who you're up against and you don't know what they're looking for. For the third recall, they decided they wanted to put myself and the other girl on film. Geraint Morris read with me and Ferdy Fairfax was there too. I read the part but I was so nervous that I was sure I'd screwed it up.

'I remember saying at the interview: "That wasn't very good, was it?" But Ferdy said reassuringly: "No, no, no. That's fine, okay."

Helen Masters as the cool Lucy Lane

'I still wasn't convinced and left thinking: "No, I've blown it. I know I've blown it."

'I walked in this frustrated daze straight to my agent's office and sat down in the chair. She said: "How did it go? How did it go?" I said: "I don't know. I was so nervous I couldn't think straight."

'Then the phone rang, literally five minutes since I had walked through the door. It was Sarah Bird and there was this horrible silence while my agent took the call. Eventually she said: "Helen." I looked up and she said: "Congratulations!"

'I was chuffed to bits. I grabbed my boyfriend and we went out for a champagne lunch to celebrate.

'I was cast just two weeks before filming began. The only drawback was I had to have my waist-length hair cut. I think my father Paul, who used to run a chain of hair salons in the Midlands, got something of a shock when he first saw me without my mane!'

With filming imminent, Helen had little opportunity for detailed research. 'But I did spend an evening with Metropolitan Police officer Jackie Molton who is the police adviser on "Prime Suspect". I went through a lot of stuff with her and she described the kind of work a Detective Inspector would be doing, the responsibilities.

'She also showed me photographs of corpses from every angle. Some were really awful. Jackie would turn the page and warn: "Go steady with those – there's some quite horrific ones." In the space of a couple of hours, I went from not really having much of an opinion about the police to having this huge respect for them. Just looking at photos of charred bodies and bodies that had been blasted out of the eighteenth storey of a block of flats in a gas explosion and had been buried in the pavement outside made me see the police in a new light. I thought they have to deal with this not every day, but on a regular basis – and they just have to get on with it.

'I said to Jackie: "What preparation do you have as a PC on the street?" She said: "None. You either deal with it, learn to deal with it or you don't do the job." '

With no police family background on which to draw ('at least not on the right side of the law' she jokes), Helen had to start from scratch. 'It's a whole world I've had to submerge myself in and get to know well. I've found that I've picked up certain traits and mannerisms and a lot of understanding of the way the police approach things. Now, when I hear about a stabbing or a similar incident, I start asking myself why did it happen, what was the motive, what lines of inquiry will the police be following up? I am far more interested and intrigued by what is happening now. I suppose playing the part of a police officer does get you thinking like one.'

And she adds mischievously: 'I've still got the warrant card so it's very tempting to go up to people and pull rank!'

Born in Coventry, Helen's schoolday antics make her the unlikeliest police recruit. She went to a fee-paying school in Leamington Spa and proceeded to wreak havoc at every opportunity. It was something straight out of St Trinian's.

'I didn't fit in at all there,' she says. 'It was a very prim and proper young ladies' school and I hated it. I rebelled against all the petty rules and regulations. They had things like posture badges which I did everything in my power not to be awarded.

'I was very badly behaved. My pranks included setting off the fire alarm, causing the classrooms to be evacuated, which in retrospect was a pretty stupid thing to do. I also stole two goldfish from the biology lab and put them in a cup that was to be presented by the headmaster at end of term prizegiving.

'The teachers were horrified at my behaviour – I was hardly the ideal pupil. The gang I hung out with were pretty uncontrollable and I'm sure we must have been a complete nightmare for the staff. Looking back, I feel rather sorry for them now. They must have been glad to see the back of me when I left after my "O" Levels.

Wycliffe's relationship with Lane is very much paternal

Lane undertakes a spot
of surveillance

'From there I went to Solihull School where, since it was only co-educational in the sixth form, I was one of just thirty-five girls among over 700 boys. But a fairly tight rein was kept on us there and I was much happier. I grew up very quickly and acted much more maturely. All the girlish pranks went out of the window.'

Although she appeared in school plays at Solihull (she was Portia in a 1980 production of *The Merchant of Venice*) and often went to the theatre at Stratford, Helen's first career choice was to be a vet.

'My father bred horses and kept cattle on our small family farm so I was brought up with animals. There's no doubt I had a privileged upbringing, but my parents are very down-to-earth people and they made sure my brother and sister and I kept our feet on the ground. My father is a very bright businessman, a working-class man made good, who at various times had a string of hairdressing salons, a series of fast-food outlets and a nightclub. That's how we ended up in that fabulous home. I used to spend most weekends and the summer holidays working with a local vet and would join him on his rounds, dealing with everything from birthing cows and pigs to gelding young colts. I got my hands dirty – it was real James Herriott stuff.

'But then I discovered that to become a vet, I needed A grades in my science subjects at "A" Level. That rather put me off and so I turned to acting. My headmaster at Solihull was very encouraging and, instead of trying to put me off, helped me to apply for drama school.'

At drama school Helen was forced to lose her Midlands accent. 'I'm not sure that's healthy, this wiping away of people's accents. It's weird when I go home and listen to my parents because I just can't speak like that any more.'

Since leaving drama school, thirty-two-year-old Helen has made guest appearances in shows such as 'Drop the Dead Donkey', 'Minder', 'Firm Friends' and 'Paul Merton – The Series (II)' as well as making a commercial for Menu Master. Her biggest role before 'Wycliffe' was as the Princess of Wales's sister, Lady Sarah Spencer, in the NBC production 'Diana – Her True Story'.

'That was a bit of a struggle,' admits Helen. 'The dialogue was full of Americanisms and we did our own thing in the end. At one point, we simply abandoned the script.'

She is much more enthusiastic about Lucy Lane. 'I like her a lot. She is very independent and very strong, a bit of a tough cookie. She's very forceful and knows when to stand her ground. People have described her as a careerist but it's a word I hate because most intelligent, well-educated people who have spent several years training and working hard for something, are careerists in that they want to succeed in their chosen vocation. I just think she's a very determined woman who wants to go all the way to the top.

'That's why she enjoys working with Wycliffe because she learns a great deal from him. In the first series, people were trying to hint at some sexual chemistry between her and Wycliffe but really he's more like a father figure to her. At first, I think he saw her as a bit of a threat – he was a little wary of her – but now he considers her to be his protegee. He gives her lots of encouragement. Besides, in the new series she acquires a regular boyfriend.

'Lucy also has huge respect for both Wycliffe and Kersey. Their three personalities are very different and so compliment one another. Kersey's approach to the job is very different from hers. He's very much a jobbing policeman whereas she's much more cerebral and will approach it from a criminal psychology point of view, through the mind of the criminal. She's interested in what makes people tick, what turns them into murderers. At the same time, she's very much "hands on" and likes to be out there at the sharp end rather than being stuck in an office.'

Helen is something of an action girl herself. During the first series, she had hoped to be able to go horse-riding on her days off but the producers banned her from any dangerous activities in case she injured herself.

'I took my riding gear down but it was all in vain. A lot of the others were learning to water ski, but they wouldn't let me do that either in case I broke anything. I was kind of miffed to start with because I thought it was a wonderful opportunity, being down in Cornwall for three months. Then I thought, "Well, I have waited so long for a break like this." So as soon as we finished shooting, I went on holiday to America and did some jet skiing to make up for it.'

However she has no desire to see Lucy become too physical, like any of the girls from "The Avengers". 'Although I'm fit through working out at the gym, I don't like violence very much. In real life my stomach turns whenever there's a hint of trouble. So I prefer Lucy to use her mind rather than start hurling suspects all over Cornwall.

'Since "Wycliffe" was my first major TV role, I was desperately keen to do well. I have to say I was completely terrified, right up to the last day of filming. But I studied Jack Shepherd a lot and he was a very calming influence.'

She has only one regret – and that is that her grandmother died in 1993. 'For years she looked out for me in one episode of this or that series, or the odd advert. Now when I'm successful at last, sadly she's not around to see it.'

AARON HARRIS

AS DETECTIVE SERGEANT ANDY DIXON

A aron Harris has one burning ambition for 1996 – to get the chance at last to act with his international movie-star uncle Richard.

'I think we're fated never to act together,' laughs Aaron. 'I was supposed to do a movie with him when I was twelve. It was called "Man in the Wilderness" and was the story of a fur trapper mauled and left for dead by a grizzly bear in 1820s Canada. It starred Uncle Richard and John Huston who was also going to direct. The script contained a flashback sequence to when the trapper was a young boy and I was supposed to do that. But then Huston decided to concentrate on acting and a new director, Richard Sarafian, came on board. Unfortunately, he decided he didn't like the flashback scene so I was out before I was even in!

Aaron Harris as the other Sergeant Dixon

'We had another near miss thirteen years later in 1984 when I played an IRA assassin in Gerald Seymour's mini series "The Glory Boys" alongside Rod Steiger and Anthony Perkins. Richard was going to play Anthony Perkins' part but had to drop out.

'Still, I've got a feeling that next year we'll finally work together in the theatre. Richard is planning his company to do three Shakespeares – *The Merchant of Venice*, *Julius Caesar* and *Macbeth*. He's intending to direct one and appear in the other two. I've signed up so, fingers crossed, the two Harrises will at last get our act together.'

Raised in County Limerick, the home of the

Harris clan, Aaron admits that it was having a famous uncle which probably first got him interested in acting. He went to the same drama school as Jack Shepherd – the Drama Centre – although, he quickly points out, 'I was some years after Jack!' The pair have also appeared together before in 'Shoot to Kill'.

'Jack played John Stalker and I was Sergeant X (he could never be named), a member of the RUC who killed a guy in a barn and sparked off the whole "shoot to kill" controversy.

Aaron's roles have tended to drift from one side of the law to the other. He has been in 'The Gentle Touch', 'The Bill', 'The Paradise Club', 'The Chief' and 'Minder' as well as enjoying a running role in the 1988 BBC police series 'Rockliffe's Folly' which was set in Dorset.

'I was Detective Constable Whitmore in that and now I've got promotion to Sergeant in "Wycliffe". So at least I'm heading in the right direction. With any luck, by the time I'm sixty I might be playing a Chief Superintendent! And of course, Richard went one better. He was Maigret.

'I also appeared in an early episode of "EastEnders", playing a character called Eamonn. When Mary, the punk girl, went on the game, I was her first client. But I couldn't go through with it so I gave her the money, threw up in the toilet of the Queen Vic and ran out!'

Aaron is aware that the last Sergeant Dixon to appear on television ended up running for over twenty-one years. While 'Wycliffe' may not have the staying power of 'Dixon of Dock Green', Aaron is confident that the series has a bright future.

'The potential is tremendous. It's so new and the characters have so much depth which can be developed. Dixon is extremely ambitious. He is not pleased that he's been overlooked for promotion in the past. His problem is that he tends to cut corners a little and that's one of the reasons he hasn't achieved promotion beyond sergeant. He's done one or two things which have upset his superiors and so he's got a couple of black marks against his name. Now he has to knuckle down and get on with it if he's to kick-start his career.'

Aaron looks forward to developing further the cameo partnership with Potter, played by Adam Barker. 'We got on so well,' he says. 'Although Adam was understandably a little nervous at the start of filming the first series, he came out of himself as we progressed and was superb. The interplay between our two characters began to develop nicely, providing odd moments of humour.'

Aaron was also captivated by Cornwall. 'It reminded me so much of the west coast of Ireland. I'll never forget the first week of filming. We were at Porthleven with driving rain, force 10 winds and the Atlantic behind us – that will stay with me as long as I live. The weather may have been inhospitable but the people couldn't have been nicer. They gave us such a welcome. I'll definitely regard it as one of my favourite parts of the country from now on.'

His research for the role of Dixon was neither conventional nor intentional. For just a few days before he began filming the first series of 'Wycliffe', Aaron suddenly found himself on the wrong side of the law. He was roughed up by uniformed police officers, mistaking him for an armed robber who had just raided a building society in Stoke Newington, London.

Dixon and Potter – a blossoming double act

'I was walking home minding my own business,' says Aaron, 'when two police cars screeched to a halt and these guys jumped out and pinned me to the wall. Eventually I discovered there'd been a robbery just up the road and I fitted the description of the suspect. I was carrying a newspaper and they thought I had a gun in it. When I explained what I was doing, it was all cleared up.'

ADAM BARKER

AS DETECTIVE CONSTABLE
IAN POTTER

T he resemblance is uncanny. At twenty-seven, Adam Barker
has the face, the build, even the hairstyle of his famous
father Ronnie at a similar age. And now Adam is following in his
father's footsteps by carving out an acting career, having made his
television debut in the first series of 'Wycliffe' little more than a
year after leaving drama school.

Just as Ronnie was a comparatively late starter in showbusiness
(he had trained as an architect and worked as a junior clerk in a
branch of the Westminster Bank for eighteen months before
taking the plunge and joining the County Theatre, Aylesbury), so
Adam did not consider a future in acting until he was half-way
through an English course at York University.

'I had no idea what I wanted to do when I was at school,' says
Adam, 'so I thought I'd go to university to study English. I joined
plenty of clubs but drama was the only thing I stuck with. I
started doing plays at university and not much work. I couldn't
get acting out of my system. In the end, I think I just came to the
conclusion that there probably wasn't much else I could do other
than act. It was the only thing I could see myself doing in life
without it becoming a real grind.

'It was a big step to take. I remember dad telling me when he
resigned from the bank that the manager had pleaded with him to
stay, saying: "You're mad. Stay five or six years here and you could
be a cashier … " So I wasn't sure how my parents would react.
Although I had always been gently steered away from
showbusiness, they had neither encouraged or discouraged me
from contemplating acting as a career. Then they came to see me

in a show at university and said how much they liked it. And when I told them what I wanted to do, they were very supportive. And they have been ever since. Dad didn't give me any advice as such. He just said if that's what I wanted, I should get out there and do it, and I agree.'

By the time Adam was born, Ronnie was already a household name. 'People think it must be difficult living in the shadow of a famous dad but because I've never known anything else, it hasn't been a problem. By the time I was aware dad was famous, he virtually had a nine-to-five existence. He was either rehearsing at Acton for "The Two Ronnies" or recording shows like "Porridge". As far as I was concerned, apart from the fact that he was out on Sundays when he recorded shows, it was an ordinary regular job, like working in a bank.

Adam Barker bears a striking resemblance to his father Ronnie

Although 'Wycliffe' is Adam's official TV debut, his eyes and the top of his head were seen in the pilot episode of the long-running BBC situation comedy 'Open All Hours' in which his father played grumpy grocer Arkwright.

'I was six at the time,' recalls Adam. 'It was only one scene. I played a little lad who had to come into the corner shop and put a note on the counter for Arkwright. The door of the shop opens, the bell rings and nothing happens until my head appears over the counter. I pass a note and don't say anything. I remember my payment for the scene was an Action Man doll!

Considering that Ronnie Barker quit showbusiness at the height of his fame, partly because of the pressures of the job, it might seem surprising that both Adam and sister Charlotte have gone into acting. 'I knew it was something I had to try,' says Adam. 'Although it took me a while to get there, I suppose given the family background, it was pretty much inevitable. The pressure of having a famous parent fades quickly once people get used to you. People in the business don't care about things like that.

'Part of the reason my father retired was that he wanted to get away from the pressure of being recognized all the time. He now lives in a little town in Oxfordshire where he's treated as a townsperson rather than a TV personality. I'm not sure that I'd want to be recognized and pointed at in the street either. I want just enough recognition for people to consider me for lots of good roles. That's my ambition.

'I've certainly been extremely lucky so far. On leaving drama school, I went to Austria and Sardinia to work alongside Susannah York in an Italian film "Princess" and then I went to Israel as part of a National Theatre tour of *The Madness of George III*. When I got back from Israel, there was a message on my answering machine from my agent about an audition for a new series. By the end of the week, Ferdy Fairfax had cast me as Potter in "Wycliffe".

'It really was perfect timing because I was just coming to the end of my eight-month run with the National and that's always a worrying time for an actor when a long job is about to finish.

'I was really nervous at first on "Wycliffe",' admits Adam, 'although it did help that we were all starting out together, all finding our feet and discovering what it was all about. It would have been even more daunting to join an established series. Television is such a different way of working to the theatre which is where, like most actors, all my training had been. The strange thing for me was the speed of television. On TV, you do a scene and then it's gone. You don't do it again. I found that weird after doing the same thing night after night in the theatre.

'You have to make sure you don't think, "Right, this is my one chance, I've really got to act it," because you'd overdo it. You've just got to let it happen. The cast and crew were tremendous and helped me no end and I learned so much just from watching an actor of the calibre of Jack Shepherd. When we did interview scenes, we would all be sitting around a table and I'd be studying the others just to see how they handled the scene.'

Apart from marking his full television debut, the role of Potter is the first time that Adam has played a policeman. 'My only previous experience of having anything to do with the police came just before I started work on "Wycliffe" when the old lady who lives next door to me in London was burgled. I heard a noise in the night, looked out of my window and saw the member of the gang who was acting as a lookout. I rang the police who came round really quickly and then I went next door with them … taking careful note to see what they did in order to pick up a few pointers for playing Potter.

'Potter's an interesting character to play. He's quite young to have made Detective Constable – sometimes it can take seven years to get from uniform to CID. But he's taken something of an academic short cut to get where he is and is now keen to go far. This time we'll see him showing a good deal more ambition. After all, he is very dedicated to his work, especially when he is tracking down something or someone on computer.'

Potter also has some nice comic moments in the series although Adam emphasizes that at this stage of his career he has no intention of emulating his father by moving into the notoriously difficult field of comedy.

'I don't want to sound picky because in this business you often have to grab what you can and do it to pay the rent. But I'm not particularly keen to get into comedy, especially not a sitcom, unless it happens to be a particularly good one. I don't want to be labelled a comic.

'I've done comedy on stage and I like to hear people laugh at me. It gives me a real buzz. But I could never be as good as dad so I've got to pick my own path. As long as I do very different things to my father, comparisons won't apply too much. But if I were to do a sitcom, dad's success would be a difficult thing to live up to.'

Adam claims that part of the physical resemblance to his father is attributable to the 'Wycliffe' catering. 'I put on three quarters of a stone filming the first series because the catering was so good. It's difficult to resist roast beef on a freezing day when you've been stuck in a field filming all morning.'

He is delighted to say that Ronnie thoroughly enjoyed the first series of 'Wycliffe'. 'He watched them all and really liked them,' enthuses Adam. He is clearly very proud of his illustrious dad. Whether Norman Stanley Fletcher would be proud of having a policeman for a son is another matter …

TIM WYLTON

AS DR FRANKS

Filming at the mortuary in Truro was definitely not one of the highspots of Tim Wylton's distinguished acting career.

'Although it looks good on screen, it really isn't the nicest place to film,' admits Tim. 'What I found slightly disconcerting was the fact that we were using the actual slab on which they put the bodies. Real corpses had been there. It was my first time in a mortuary and I kept looking around at all these strange bottles which, thankfully, were covered so that you couldn't see the heart or whatever was inside. Also, while we were there, we could see them wheeling in bodies in the background. It could be a little off-putting.

'Yet the young guy who lays out the bodies there absolutely loves his job. He gave me a complete rundown. He said that sometimes when the bodies first come in, they stink a bit but you get used to it. I thought: "My God, this isn't the job for me!"'

Tim's main source of research for the role was a book by the eminent police pathologist Keith Simpson. 'That gave me an excellent insight into the work of a pathologist, the sort of things they have to deal with and what they're looking for. We decided that Franks would be fond of a drink. It seems that a lot of pathologists are – it's an antidote to the awful job they do, looking at dead bodies. Pathologists also tend to be very jolly with a macabre sense of humour and so in The Scapegoat, Franks took great delight in describing the contents of the dead man's stomach.'

Now fifty-five, Tim was bitten by the acting bug at an early age. 'I was born in Wales but my parents sent me to school in Scotland since for some reason they thought it was good for me to have a

Scottish education. So there I was with a North Walian accent having to wear a kilt! Anyway I started appearing in school plays and I enjoyed hearing the sound of audience laughter so I began to think: "I wonder if I can get away with doing this for the rest of my life."'

He has been in constant demand ever since, from playing the gormless Eric in Jack Rosenthal's 1969 comedy 'The Dustbinmen' to the more recent success of 'A Bit of a Do.' 'Wycliffe' gave him the opportunity to renew his acquaintance with producer Geraint Morris.

Tim Wylton as the jovial police pathologist, Franks

'Geraint and I go way back,' says Tim, 'to "Juliet Bravo" and "Casualty". The second series of "Wycliffe" was being filmed at the same time as I was appearing in *The Merry Wives of Windsor* for the National Theatre in London. Geraint was very good about it and scheduled my scenes as Franks around the London production.

'I've been lucky in that I've always managed to keep in work. I find that short, round blokes like myself get more work than tall, thin ones. We're officially called "character actors" but some of us christen ourselves "grotesques"! Funnily enough, I've never played either a policeman or a medical man before so "Wycliffe" is something of a first. In fact over the years, I've not had many suit parts. Of course, some series turn out to be less successful than others: I was in "The Bretts", which was not a success. I also appeared in the BBC's "Lifeboat", which is where I got the mac which Franks wears.'

Tim's full name is Tim Wylton-Higginson but RADA said that was too long and advised him to shorten it to Tim Wylton. One of his four children is actor Huw Higginson who plays PC George Garfield in 'The Bill'. When he was 12, Huw appeared alongside his father in the Royal Shakespeare Company production of *'Henry IV, Part II'*.

'I've been in a couple of episodes of "The Bill"', says Tim, 'but Garfield hasn't had to arrest me yet! But I'm sure Huw's working on it … '

There was one lighter moment during filming at Truro mortuary. Tim recalls: 'Most television companies do Christmas outtakes which they play back for a bit of fun – rather like "It'll Be Alright On The Night". We decided to do one with a lady extra who was playing a corpse lying on the slab in the mortuary. We got her to lie there and suddenly go 'Boo!' for the Christmas tape. She did that and then we came to do the scene for real as part of "Wycliffe". The camera panned round and as it moved in on her, she suddenly sat up and went "Boo!" again. We had to explain to her: "No, no, no, we've got that. You don't actually wake up and say 'Boo!' in the Wycliffe script." Eventually she got the message!'

WYCLIFFE INVESTIGATES

THE FOUR JACKS

Murders didn't happen in Porthellis. They took place in London, Liverpool, even Plymouth, but not the picturesque Cornish coastal village, a community which had never witnessed anything more heinous than the odd case of illegal parking in the holiday season. And that wasn't the locals – it was trippers. But as waves lashed against the rocks and seagulls battled overhead against the prevailing westerlies, Kersey and Lane found themselves investigating a callous shooting. It wasn't yet a murder case but the victim's wounds were so serious as to suggest that it would be only a matter of time before it was.

Transmission date: 24 July 1994
Writer: Edward Canfor-Dumas
Director: Ferdinand Fairfax

SUPPORTING CAST
David Cleeve - Bill Nighy
Patricia Cleeve - Susan Wooldridge
Gerald Prout - Roger Sloman
Barbara Prout - Georgine Anderson
PC Pearce - Tim Treslove
Milli - Pandora Ormsby Gore
Paul Redman - Rupam Maxwell
Professor Faber - Nicholas Gecks

Shot by an unknown assailant, Celia Dawe is stretchered from the cottage

The victim, a young student named Celia Dawe, was working on a local archaeological dig. Her body had been discovered early that morning by fellow student Paul Redman. Calling at the tiny cottage she rented, he had let himself in with a key kept under a flower pot. She was a notoriously late riser and he had gone to wake her. Finding her still in bed, he had opened the curtains in an attempt to rouse her. When this had proved unsuccessful, he had shaken her gently … until he realized that her pillow was soaked in blood.

While Miss Dawe was rushed off by helicopter to Plymouth, an incident room was set up in a nearby hall. An early visitor was the tall, distinguished David Cleeve, owner of the cottage the girl was staying in. He had come to see whether he could be of any assistance.

'Did you know her?' asked Lane. 'Celia Dawe?'

'Er, no, not personally, no. I only knew them vaguely, en masse. The students.'

'How did you come to be involved in the dig, Mr Cleeve?'

'Oh, aerial photography, apparently. They spotted the outline of an ancient settlement on my land and Professor Faber wrote to me asking if they could investigate and before I knew it, we'd been invaded. We're quite private, my wife and I, so it was a bit of a shock having all those young people setting up camp – within hailing distance of the house, almost.'

'You offered them the accommodation?'

'Yes. Living under canvas seemed just too primitive to me, even for students. Plus I have holiday properties and it's out of season.'

'And do you know how Celia Dawe came to have the cottage by herself?'

Cleeve shrugged his shoulders. 'No. I assume they tossed for it, or something.'

Celia Dawe's chances of survival were 60-40. But even then, she would be of little help to the police. For she had suffered severe brain damage. Lane tried to piece together details of the girl's background. Paul Redman, who had clearly been very fond of her, painted a picture of a quiet, serious girl, an impression confirmed by Professor Faber out at the site of the dig. However the Professor did produce one tasty morsel to whet Lane's appetite – David Cleeve was better known as the celebrated author Peter Stride.

Back at the incident room, Wycliffe had arrived. Wandering among his team, he outlined the evidence to date.

'So,' he began, 'MMO – means, motive and opportunity. Well, the means was obviously a gun – probably a handgun, judging by the wound – and probably using a silencer since the house-to-house hasn't turned up anyone who heard a shot. Motive is trickier. Traces on the bedding suggest sex had taken place quite recently but how soon before the shooting we don't know. So whoever was there is for now either a prime suspect or at least a key witness.'

'So it's a crime of passion, sir,' suggested Kersey.

Wycliffe remained non-committal. 'Right now we've got to keep an open mind. What've you found out about her, Lucy?'

'Not a great deal. To all intents and purposes she was a quiet, well-liked, studious … student.'

'By day,' interrupted Kersey.

'That's right,' said Wycliffe. 'By day. And if she was leading a double life, who knows what'll turn up if we dig deep enough? So, more to do there, Lucy. Okay? Right. Opportunity. All we've got so far is a light-coloured Metro-type vehicle seen leaving the village around three in the morning.'

'The gunman?' queried Lane.

'Maybe, maybe not,' answered Wycliffe, deep in thought. 'But from past experience, the probability is that whoever tried to kill Celia Dawe lives locally. So we start by tracing that car.'

'The Cleeves have got one,' revealed the local bobby, PC Pearce. 'A Metro.' This was indeed food for thought.

One thing still puzzled Lane. 'Redman says he found Celia lying on her back under the covers. Which means her front was to the door. So why did the bullet hit her near the back of her head, just about her left ear, the side that was to the wall?'

'She had to be that way round when she was hit,' said Kersey, 'and then moved.'

'By whom?'

'There's only two possibilities,' stated Wycliffe, 'realistic ones that is. She was moved by whoever was with her or whoever shot her – assuming they're two different people, of course.'

Lane remained perplexed. 'That interview with Cleeve. Something about it didn't feel, I don't know. It's when he came in. He didn't ask any questions about what had happened – who it was who'd been shot, or which cottage or anything. He just offered his help straight off.'

'Perhaps he'd already been told,' said Kersey.

'Perhaps,' mused Lane.

Wycliffe decided it was time for a chat with the mysterious Mr

Wycliffe discovers the true identity of David Cleeve (Bill Nighy)

Cleeve and drove out to Roscrowgy, the Cleeves' impressive house overlooking the sea. Writing books was clearly a profitable business. Wycliffe inquired about the Metro. Cleeve's attractive wife Patricia said it was hers and that on the day in question it had been in Falmouth for its annual service. Wycliffe asked to be shown into the study, on the pretence of wanting to see where the great man worked. In truth, he wanted to speak to Cleeve alone.

'Peter Stride's supposed to be notoriously reclusive,' said Wycliffe.

'Lose your anonymity and you lose your freedom.'

'Is that why there are no photos of you on your books?'

'Yes.'

'So why agree to all these students digging up your land?'

'Well, they don't know me as Peter Stride – only as David Cleeve. Besides, I find the past fascinating.'

Without changing pitch, Wycliffe went for the jugular. 'Were you sleeping with Celia Dawe, Mr Cleeve?'

Cleeve was outraged. 'What?'

Wycliffe continued regardless. 'We believe she was with a man the night she was shot. She was in one of your properties alone. Do you have a key?'

'Well yes, of course.'

Cleeve protested his innocence. Wycliffe arranged for the collection of the clothes Cleeve was wearing on the night of the shooting.

Just as the net seemed to be closing in on Cleeve, there was another shooting. This time it was fatal. A middle-aged man, identified from credit cards he was carrying as Roger Kitson, was gunned down by a single rifle shot to the back of the head while walking his dog on a deserted stretch of beach near Newquay. Time of death was later established as ten o'clock in the morning.

'Coincidence. Two shootings in two days,' said Lane.

'Don't like coincidences,' replied Wycliffe brusquely. 'But it looks like two different weapons. Ballistics just confirmed Celia was shot with a handgun, a nine-millimetre. So for the time being, we treat these two shootings as separate.'

Lane and DC Potter searched Kitson's shabby room. They unearthed a series of bus passes, credit cards, drivers' licences and passports, offering different identities. Arthur Mitchell, Ronald Clark, Francis Collins, Edward Zennon, Roger Kitson. He had more names than Lloyd's. Lane also discovered a red, heart-shaped metal brooch with a large letter 'J' in the centre. It seemed to signify the Jack of Hearts.

Meanwhile Cleeve had decided to come clean to Wycliffe and Kersey about his relationship with Celia Dawe. 'She wasn't the prettiest of the bunch but there was something about her I suppose,' he sighed. 'Anyway, I found her attractive and I made sure she got the single cottage. Then it was just a question of dropping by one evening and, well, playing the famous novelist card, I'm afraid. It's stood me in rather good stead over the years. I can't seem to help it, Superintendent. There are some men – and I'm ashamed to say I'm one – who seem compelled to sleep with virtually every woman they meet. Proving something, I suppose. Deeply insecure, afraid of death or something. Anyway, there it is.'

'Does your wife know?' asked Wycliffe.

'She has the grace to regard my adventures as the price of my "genius", I suppose. From my wife I get comfort, security, a sense of continuity. But from the others – you name it.'

'And you were with Celia two night ago?' pressed Wycliffe. 'What happened?'

'It was utterly bizarre,' replied Cleeve, shaking his head. 'She was – she is – a young woman full of energy. And we were in bed when she suddenly rolled on top of me and gave this great jerk and went limp. Well, I thought I'd done my stuff, you know, and lay there holding her, but after a while when she didn't move or say anything, I began to be a bit alarmed. And then the pillow seemed wet. So I turned on the lamp and there was blood everywhere. I ... I just couldn't understand it.'

'You hadn't heard anything? A shot?'

'No, she was really quite passionate ... when aroused.'

'What time was this?'

'Just after three.'

'Why didn't you call for an ambulance?'

'I know you don't think much of me, gentlemen. I don't think much of myself. That's just how I react to crises. I don't know why.'

'Who do you think might have done it, Mr Cleeve?'

'I've no idea – unless, unless they were aiming at me.'

'So how many women have you slept with since you moved down here, Mr Cleeve?' inquired Kersey, his voice betraying a hint of envy.

'It's been over twenty years, Inspector.' He hazarded a guess. 'Well, three-hundred?'

With the possibility of so many irate husbands or boyfriends on the loose, Cleeve thought his perilous position warranted police protection. Wycliffe was not convinced.

After a fruitless session checking Kitson's aliases on the computer, Lane joined Wycliffe and Kersey to re-enact the shooting of Celia Dawe at the cottage. Kersey was by no means dismayed to find that he was acting out the part of Cleeve with Lane playing Celia. Under Wycliffe's watchful eye, they climbed on the bed together and Kersey lay on his back with Lane astride him. It was never like this at police school.

'Right,' said Wycliffe standing by the staircase, 'now we know the shot came from here and that Celia was hit behind the left ear. According to Cleeve, she was above him and then he turned her over on to her back and covered her up.'

He imitated the firing of a gun. 'Bang! So Doug, what do you do?'

'I get dressed and leg it, sir,' answered Kersey, turning Lane over.

'Which means … ?' pursued Wycliffe

' … I'm virtually certain to have blood on my clothes.'

'That's right.'

'But if you'd shot me … ?' interjected Lane.

' … I'd get dressed first,' said Kersey. 'So no bloodstains at all.'

Wycliffe was quietly satisfied. 'Forensic's going to make interesting reading, isn't it?'

The forensic report was soon available. Cleeve's clothing revealed significant traces of the victim's blood.

'So Cleeve's out of the frame then,' said Kersey.

Wycliffe was hedging his bets. 'Not necessarily.'

Kersey couldn't see the problem. 'Well, unless he went outside in the nude, shot her, then came back in, rolled about in her blood then got dressed again!'

Even Wycliffe was forced to concede that such a scenario seemed unlikely. But he remained convinced that Cleeve held the key to the case and ordered a thorough investigation into his background.

'I want you to find out everything that you can, and I mean everything, about this man – where he was born, what school he went to, the colour of his first bike, the lot. And let's see if this Metro being serviced story checks out.'

Wycliffe didn't like Cleeve. He despised his outlook on life, especially his morals – or rather the lack of them. He decided to have another chat with Mrs Cleeve. She said that at the time of the Kitson shooting, her husband was walking off a hangover. Wycliffe then asked her what she was doing on the Monday night when Celia Dawe was shot.

'I can assure you, Mr Wycliffe,' she replied calmly, 'if I'd been cursed with a jealous nature, I'd be guilty of mass murder by now. I was here, in bed, probably asleep and no, I don't have anyone to confirm that. Discretion – that's the *sine qua non* of these arrangements, oh, and the blind eye. David seems to think that being "famous" and "creative" means he doesn't have to live by the same rules as other people.'

'Why do you stay?'

'Oh, the heart, Mr Wycliffe. The heart.'

Wycliffe was none the wiser. He had bowed to Cleeve's request for protection but had assigned PC Pearce to the task principally to find out as much as possible about Cleeve. In return, the author had written down a list of his lovers. It read like a Cornwall telephone directory and included Milli, his secretary for the past two years. Cleeve was curious to know more about the death of Kitson, particularly since Wycliffe had described him as an ex-army type of similar age to Cleeve. In the wake of the discovery of the Jack of Hearts brooch among the dead man's belongings, Lane ordered all bridge clubs within a thirty-mile radius to be contacted in a bid to uncover his real identity. Just then Potter broke in excitedly.

'Ma'am. I think we got something here. This chap, birdwatcher, was parked here overlooking the beach and remembers seeing a yellow Metro a couple of hours before the murder.'

'A Metro? Did he get the number?'

'Yep. He'd heard about it on the radio. We ran it through PNC – it's registered to a Mrs Barbara Prout. Plus, I checked and we've already interviewed the driver, Gerald Prout.'

'Have we indeed?'

'Coincidence?'

'The Super doesn't believe in coincidences.'

Wycliffe and Lane wasted no time in going to interview Gerald Prout. The door was answered by his wife, a somewhat belligerent woman of around sixty. Although she allowed them in, she made it abundantly clear that they were not welcome.

'We're investigating a car,' said Wycliffe, entering the lounge. 'A yellow Metro has been traced to this address. Where is your husband, Mrs Prout?'

'He's away on business,' she answered curtly.

'What sort of business?'

'He's a salesman.'

'Has he been in touch at all?'

'Yesterday, he rang me yesterday. Why?'

'We do need to talk to your husband as a matter of some urgency, Mrs Prout. Someone saw his car at the scene of a crime. Now, if we could ... '

Before he could finish, Mrs Prout had interrupted. 'My husband's never been in trouble in his life.'

Wycliffe was facing an uphill struggle. Mrs Prout eventually volunteered that her husband had phoned from a call box and had not given an address for the farmhouse where he was staying. She added that she had been forced to surrender her driving licence six months ago through ill health. Wycliffe sensed she could – or would – not help any further but threw out the customary parting shot.

'When you do next hear from your husband, Mrs Prout, I'd be grateful if you'd contact me straightaway.'

'I'll not be here,' she replied.

Wycliffe was taken aback. 'I beg your pardon?'

'I'm going away. They've tried to put me off again of course, but I'll not be stopped. I'm going to London.'

Wycliffe was now completely lost. 'I don't understand ... '

She went into the bedroom and produced a letter from a file. 'I had a letter from them this morning. Some office nobody.' She handed it to Wycliffe. 'Here, have a look.'

Wycliffe read part of it aloud. '"The Home Secretary regrets he will be unable to see you at the present time."'

Mrs Prout became more agitated than ever. 'I'll camp outside his bloody house all night if I have to, ill or not. I've rung the newspapers and the telly people. They'll all be there to see what happens. He's got to see me.'

Wycliffe stared at the wall behind her. There was a framed photograph of four young soldiers, each with a picture playing card beneath – the Jack of Clubs, the Jack of Spades, the Jack of Diamonds and the Jack of Hearts. He focused on one of the names. 'Jonathan Welsh. Was he your brother, Mrs Prout?' He turned to Lane. 'The Shotton House killings, 1960. Jonathan Welsh was hanged for shooting a policeman.'

'Murdered,' interrupted Mrs Prout, 'murdered by the state on the fifteenth of April, 1961. They said at the trial there were two sets of fingerprints on the gun. He had a gun. But my brother never pulled the trigger. He couldn't have done. If you'd known what he was like ... It was Larkin did that – John Larkin – and the other two lied to save their skins. But what's the good of telling you? You're not interested. Just like all the rest of them. Too busy trying to protect your precious legal system.'

Wycliffe studied the photographs again. 'Cross. The Jack of Hearts.'

'Roger John Cross,' said Mrs Prout. 'He let my innocent brother hang, while he got off with a few years in jail. Do you call that justice? Do you?'

Wycliffe put two and two together. 'Roger Cross is dead, Mrs Prout. He was shot and killed two days ago.' At last, he had discovered Roger Kitson's true identity.

Wycliffe and Lane walked to the car. 'Right,' he said, 'call HQ. Get them to put the chopper up. Sweep the area within a twenty-mile radius, more if it's possible. Looking for a yellow Metro parked outside a farmhouse.'

'Nothing more precise?' queried Lane.

'No.' Wycliffe was deep in thought. 'Four Jacks … Welsh was hanged, Cross is dead.

'So what happened to the others, Jack Shirley and John Larkin?'

Wycliffe took a long breath. 'Let's hope we find them before Prout does.'

Back at the incident room, further information began to emerge about the four young men known as the Four Jacks. Their nickname sprang from the fact that they all had Jack or John in their name – Roger John Cross, John Larkin, Jack Shirley and Jonathan Welsh. Wycliffe was extremely anxious to ascertain the whereabouts of Shirley and Larkin. Lane quickly provided one of the answers.

'Sir, Jack Shirley's dead as well. According to CRO, he died of a heart attack in prison, eight years ago.'

'And then there was one,' pondered Wycliffe. 'Larkin.'

The helicopter managed to locate the Metro by the old Engine House at Borlase Mine, some ten miles away. Wycliffe and Lane rushed to the scene. There was no sign of Prout.

'Reckon he's there?' asked Lane.

'Well let's wait for Firearms to find out,' said Wycliffe.

'Well, bad news – they're on another shout. So we either play the hero or wait.'

Gerald Prout (Roger Sloman) gunning for revenge

For Wycliffe, it was no contest. 'We'll wait.'

Wycliffe and Lane had no option but to spend an uncomfortable night in the car before the Firearms Unit arrived at dawn the following morning. Still there was no sign of life. The assault team were taking no chances. They surrounded the engine house and then burst through the front door while Wycliffe and Lane watched from a distance. No luck. The bird had flown the nest. But he had left behind some nine-millimetre ammunition – the type used in the shooting of Celia Dawe.

The search into Cleeve's past finally paid off. David Paul Cleeve had been born at Bristol on 5 September 1931 but had died on 12 October 1944 at Exeter General Hospital from multiple injuries sustained in a road traffic accident the same day. The man now calling himself David Cleeve was really John Larkin, the Jack of Clubs. It didn't take Sherlock Holmes to deduce that Prout was heading for Roscrowgy to finish off the last of the Four Jacks.

At Roscrowgy, Cleeve was growing increasingly restless, all the more so when his minder, Pearce, revealed that the suspect for the shootings was a man named Prout. During the dash by car, Wycliffe radioed Pearce, warning him not to allow Cleeve out of the house under any circumstances, but the frightened Cleeve was determined to make a run for it.

Wycliffe's car screeched to a halt in the driveway. He leaped out and banged on the front door. As he did so, he heard a gunshot from the rear of the house.

'Round the back!' he yelled to the Firearms Unit.

Just then Prout appeared with the gun. He and Wycliffe froze. Wycliffe calmly tried to defuse the situation.

'Stay where you are Gerald! Keep the gun pointing at the ground, don't lift it, whatever you do Gerald, don't lift the gun.'

Prout obeyed the instructions.

'That's it,' continued Wycliffe, his voice betraying few signs of a pounding heart, 'it's over, Gerald. It's over. We're police. You don't want to shoot at us, do you?'

Prout eased his grip on the gun.

'That's it,' said Wycliffe, 'drop the gun, let your fingers go … That's it. Let them go. Drop it.'

Prout dropped the gun and was immediately overpowered. A distraught Pearce emerged from behind him.

'I didn't get a chance,' gabbled Pearce to his superior officer. 'I couldn't … '

'Save it for the inquiry,' said Wycliffe.

Prout had broken into the house and shot Cleeve in his study. There, Patricia cradled her dead husband in her arms, sobbing uncontrollably. Wycliffe was angry. He should have been able to prevent Cleeve's death.

In the interview room at the station, Prout looked at a photograph of the Four Jacks.

'Took a long time to find him. Covered his tracks real well. Cleeve, Stride, who'd have thought it?'

'Why now?' asked Wycliffe.

'Larkin should have hanged thirty years ago,' said Prout, unrepentant.

'So you wanted to see justice done, huh?'

Prout faced his interrogator. 'You married, Mr Wycliffe? See they didn't just kill that young policeman and Jonny, you know. They killed us too. Our marriage. Our life together. And they've finally killed Barbs for real.'

'Mrs Prout?'

'Yeh, she's dying, Mr Wycliffe. Cancer. Only got a few months left. Hearing that was the last straw, you know.'

'So what about Celia Dawe, where's the justice for her?'

'Yeh, I'm sorry about that – they moved, didn't they?' He looked down at the desk in shame. 'Shouldn't have done that. Didn't mean it.' He paused before reverting his gaze to Wycliffe. 'But it's always the innocent who suffer, isn't it?'

Celia Dawe died shortly afterwards without regaining consciousness.

THE DEAD FLAUTIST

THE DEAD FLAUTIST
Transmission date: 31 July 1994
Writer: Steve Trafford
Director: Martyn Friend

SUPPORTING CAST
Guy Bottrell - David Bamber
Hugh Bottrell - Jeremy Clyde
Paul Bottrell - Ben Mangham
Cynthia Bottrell - Susan Fleetwood
Mrs Christopher - Mary Wimbush
Jean Lander - Emily Hamilton
Edith Lander - Susan Derrick
Steven Lander - James Faulkner
Fox - Ian Keith
Carter - Ken Watson
Jed - Garry Scanlan
WPC Angela - Dee Sadler
Landlord - David Sterne

The Bottrells were one of Cornwall's most distinguished families. Devout Catholics with a family motto of *'Fides ad mortem'* (Keep faith unto death), they dated back centuries. Sometimes they had suffered for their religion. George Ignatius Bottrell, chaplain to Queen Mary, had been burnt at the stake in the sixteenth century as a heretic. The current occupants of Bottrell Hall, Lord Hugh and Lady Cynthia Bottrell, were not subject to such quaint customs and had maintained the estate to a high standard. Theirs was the envy of many stately homes. Then the idyllic scene was shattered by tragedy. The body of the estate manager, a thirty-five-year-old bachelor by the name of Tony Miller, was found in his cottage by a local girl, Jean Lander, out on an early Saturday morning walk. She had noticed the cottage door swinging open in the wind and, hearing Miller's dog whining, stepped inside to investigate. Miller had died from gunshot wounds, apparently self-inflicted. 'Nasty way to go,' remarked Kersey, 'playing lollipop with your own shotgun.'

Closer analysis suggested that it might not have been suicide after all. The shotgun had been pressed beneath the dead man's chin but, given the angle of entry, his arms might not have been long enough to have pulled the trigger.

Wycliffe met the Bottrells in the sitting room at the hall. Lord Hugh's brother, Guy, and teenage son, Paul, were also present. Whereas Lord Hugh was courteous and softly spoken, Guy was abrasive to the point of arrogance. Wycliffe established that Miller had been employed there for some seven years. He tried to obtain some background about the dead man's lifestyle.

'He was quite a solitary chap,' said Hugh.

Guy put it more forcefully. 'Bloody refugee from life – just the sort to come unstuck and top himself. Seen it in the army time enough. Miserable cove, Miller.'

Neither did Lady Cynthia show much respect for the departed. 'Pickled more often than not. Wasn't he, Hugh?'

A fragile marriage –
Lady Cynthia and Lord
Hugh Bottrell (Susan
Fleetwood and Jeremy
Clyde)

Wycliffe asked whether anyone had heard a gunshot on the Friday night. Lady Cynthia said she was in bed all evening with a migraine; Lord Hugh was travelling back by train from a debate in the House of Lords; Paul was in his room watching a Sylvester Stallone film on television; but Guy was unable to account for his movements. Nor did he see any reason why he should.

Lane interviewed the household staff, among them estate foreman George Carter. 'Miller didn't mix well,' said Carter. 'Lads is always down the Botty Arms, Fridays, darts night. But he'd never show. Rum sort of chap.'

'Girlfriends?' inquired Lane.

Carter gave a hearty laugh. 'Not what you'd call a ladies' man. Don't get me wrong. I liked the fella. But he were a bit soft, that's all. Tell the truth, he didn't know if he was Artha or Martha!'

Back at Miller's cottage, Lane relayed the rumour that the dead man was gay.

'That's interesting,' said Kersey. 'There was a name and number on his phone pad. Lizzie. I thought it might be a girlfriend. Could be his sister, I suppose.'

'I had a mention of a maid up at the hall name of Lizzie,' said Lane. 'Lizzie Biddick. Gone to London, according to the housekeeper.'

While Criminal Records Office checks were run on the Bottrells, Wycliffe and Kersey went to interview Jean Lander, the girl who had found the body. Her oppressive solicitor father insisted on answering most of the questions on her behalf. When she did manage to get a word in, she said that she had found the body at around half past nine on the Saturday morning. The look on the girl's face and her edgy mannerisms told Wycliffe that she was lying. By now, Wycliffe was definitely looking at a case of murder. The pathology report confirmed that Miller's death could not possibly have been suicide. The entry wound was below the chin and out through the back of the head. Given the shotgun's length, Miller couldn't possibly have achieved that angle of fire holding the gun himself.

That afternoon, Dixon and a team of uniformed policemen hauled a bag from a well near Miller's cottage. The bag contained explicit photographs of Lizzie Biddick and a return coach ticket to London dated for the Friday. The ticket had not been used. A call to the number on Miller's pad revealed that Lizzie had indeed been expected in London last Friday but had not turned up.

'I had another word with the housekeeper,' said Lane. 'Her room is next to Biddick's. Late last Thursday night she heard her come in, bang about for five minutes, then leave again in a hurry.'

'She didn't see her?' asked Wycliffe.

'No, sir.'

'Maybe Biddick was having a scene with Miller,' suggested Kersey. 'She finds out he's cowboying around, they row and she shoots him. She could've wiped the gun clean, took his hand, laid his prints all over it, to look like suicide, then run home, packed a bag and dropped it down the well to fake a disappearance.'

Wycliffe was not convinced. 'Why the photos in the bag of her – naked?' He ordered the whole area to be searched thoroughly, expecting to find the body of Lizzie Biddick.

In the meantime, he wanted to see whether Guy Bottrell's memory had returned. Cornering him on a clay-pigeon shoot, Wycliffe asked him where he was between nine thirty and eleven o'clock the previous Friday night.

Guy hedged his reply. 'Look, this is all rather ... awkward. I was with somebody ... '

'Would you mind telling me who? Were you with Lizzie Biddick that night?'

'Lizzie Biddick? Good God no, of course not!'

Lady Cynthia strode over, a shotgun slung across her shoulder. 'Guy was with me, Superintendent.'

Wycliffe shot her a quizzical look. 'I thought you said you were alone that night, madam, with a migraine?'

'Yes, I said that. It wasn't true. You see, my husband knows nothing about this.'

Wycliffe decided to take another look at the murder site. He was alarmed to discover Lord Hugh rummaging through Miller's desk. Confronted with the fact that fingerprints other than Miller's had turned up all over the cottage – kitchen, bathroom, even bedroom – Lord Hugh confessed that he and Miller had been lovers virtually from the day Miller first came to work for him. On his way back, Wycliffe offered a lift to Jean Lander and Paul Bottrell. It was no chance encounter. Eventually Jean admitted that she had discovered Miller's body not on the Saturday morning while walking alone, but on the Friday night while walking through the woods with Paul. She had concocted the story for fear of her father's reaction.

'You don't know him,' she told Wycliffe. 'He goes mad if I'm out late. He always thinks I'm out with Paul. He knows we see each other ... '

Wycliffe issued a paternal admonishment. 'You've been a very irresponsible young lady.'

'I know. I'm sorry. Sorry. Please don't tell my father. He'll kill me. I mean it.'

Wycliffe was more concerned with solving the case than telling tales out of school. 'Was there anything else you saw that night?'

Eager to assist in a bid to win Wycliffe's silence, Jean gave the question serious thought. 'There might have been something. I don't know, it was dark.'

'You saw someone?'

'Not saw. Heard. A man – running through the woods. I didn't see his face. I only saw him for a moment. We were running – I was frightened.'

Kersey was gainfully employed trying to find out who had taken the photos of Lizzie Biddick. They were more than just happy snaps – they bore the mark of a professional or at least an enthusiastic amateur. Inquiries at Kersey's favourite source of information, the local pub, revealed that Mr Lander ran a small photographic club with a studio in the old boathouse down by the estuary.

As Kersey knocked on the door, he was met by Lander emerging from the darkroom with a contact sheet.

'Private club is it, sir?' asked Kersey pointedly.

Lander was visibly defensive. 'Just a group of amateur enthusiasts.'

'And what sort of pictures get their juices flowing, Mr Lander? These enthusiasts. Landscapes? Still life? Full frontal?'

Lander was taken aback. 'I beg your pardon?'

'We're looking for a young lady. Miss Lizzie Biddick.' He handed Lander the photographs of Lizzie. 'Do you know her?'

Lander remained evasive. 'Lizzie who … ?'

'Do you recognize her?' persisted Kersey.

Lander examined the prints. 'I don't think … '

'Yes, it's difficult, isn't it?' said Kersey, continuing on the offensive. 'They all look different in their birthday suits, don't they?'

Lander surrendered. 'Yes. It's Lizzie Biddick.'

'Did one of your fellow enthusiasts take these. Or was it you?'

'I took them,' sighed Lander. 'Look, I know what you're thinking, Inspector, but Lizzie had ambitions to become a model. She wanted a portfolio of photographs.'

'She paid you to take them, did she?'

'No. No, I was interested in doing some life studies ... '

'Ah, that's what they are, is it?' said Kersey with more than a hint of sarcasm.

'She needed the photos to show agents,' protested Lander. He was fighting a losing battle.

The discovery of Lizzie Biddick's naked body in a clump of bushes near the mouth of the estuary made Lander's position as a pillar of the community even more precarious. Her neck had been broken and the absence of any clothing nearby suggested that she had been killed elsewhere and dumped there.

'A blow to the neck with a blunt weapon,' pronounced Franks examining Lizzie's body in the mortuary. 'Main artery ruptured. Massive haemorrhage to the brain. Sometime last Wednesday or Thursday. Just before Mr Miller ... And there are fibres. Could be her own clothes. Could be she grabbed at her assailant.'

'Any other injury?' asked Wycliffe.

'No sign of close encounters of a sexual nature. She was an extremely healthy woman.'

Lander was brought in for questioning.

'I took some photographs of the girl. That was all,' he told Wycliffe.

'Did you and she have any other sort of relationship?'

'No, of course not. What do you take me for?'

Some questions are best left unanswered.

'Were you aware,' said Wycliffe, 'that Lizzie Biddick was a close friend of Tony Miller's?'

'No. She may have mentioned him now and again.'

'Did you take any photos of Tony Miller?' asked Kersey. 'Any ... life studies?'

'No. These photographs have only an aesthetic and artistic interest to me.'

'Artistic!' exclaimed Kersey. 'Frankly, Mr Lander, some of these'd make a pornographer

Kersey awaits developments with Steven Lander (James Faulkner)

blush.'

'That may be your judgement. I can't be responsible for other people's perverse and limited imaginations, Inspector.'

'We do have some other photographs of Lizzie Biddick,' said Wycliffe, 'which were taken more recently. At the place where her body was discovered. Ms Biddick was found dead earlier today. When did you last see her?'

'I don't know – last week sometime.'

'Did you kill Lizzie Biddick?' asked Kersey.

'No. I did not,' responded Lander angrily. 'Understand plain English? I have not, could not, did not … kill Lizzie Biddick.'

Wycliffe was not sure whether to believe him and decided to have another go at Lander's daughter Jean. He asked her whether it was her father that she had seen running away from Miller's cottage and whether that was why she had lied about finding the body. Jean remained adamant about being unable to identify the fleeing man. Wycliffe turned to Lander's wife, Edith.

'Mrs Lander, were you aware that your husband was taking photographs of Lizzie Biddick?'

'I suspected there was someone – he has an interest in that kind of thing.'

'Pornography?' asked Wycliffe.

'He calls it "art".'

'Have you any reason to suppose that something else was going on between your husband and Lizzie Biddick?'

'No.'

'Would you say your husband is a violent man, Mrs Lander?'

As Edith hesitated, Jean leapt to her feet. 'Tell him mother! Tell the truth about him for once!'

'Quiet Jean!' said her mother.

Jean would not be silenced. 'He treats her like dirt. He's so jealous. She can't even go to the shops but he accuses her of meeting a man. Shouting and screaming at her. And he asked me to do it – to pose for some pictures. I told him I didn't want to and he said I mustn't tell you he'd asked or, or he'd stop me ever seeing Paul again.'

For all his faults, however, Edith Lander did not believe that her husband was capable of murder.

Lane was concentrating on the Bottrells. She found Lady Cynthia in the Hall's private chapel arranging flowers and asked her how she coped with Lord Hugh's relationship with Tony Miller. Could her resentment have been a motive for murder?

Lady Cynthia dismissed the idea out of hand. 'I've put up with Hugh's peccadilloes for twenty years. One learns to live with such things. I am my husband's wife. Loyalty to country, church and family is the true Trinity, Inspector.'

'And yet you were with Guy Bottrell the night Mr Miller died?'

'Since he has chosen to tell you that, I'm not in a position to deny it.'

'And I take it your husband knows nothing of this?'

'Hugh has always been entirely oblivious to everything save his own infatuations.'

'Including the fact that you sleep with his brother?'

'Some things one has to do. And one can only pray for forgiveness. But I repeat, I am my husband's wife, and that ... that I shall take to my grave, as I vowed before God to do.'

At the incident room, Wycliffe, Lane and Kersey weighed up the evidence so far. Lander certainly seemed favourite. He had no alibi for the time of either killing and his family said he could be violent. One thing puzzled Wycliffe. Why would someone so meticulous as Lander have put the photographs in the bag when he must have known they would ultimately be traced back to him?

'Panicked,' suggested Kersey.

'Yes – well then why kill Miller two days later?' asked Lane.

'Afraid he knew too much. Lizzie and Miller were friends, probably lovers. Jealousy?'

Wycliffe didn't buy it. 'What did she say, Lady Cynthia, when you put Guy's alibi to her?'

'She confirmed it,' said Lane.

Wycliffe became uncharacteristically animated. 'No, no, no. What did she say?'

Lane was shaken by his outburst. She consulted her notes. 'Er … She said … "If he's chosen to tell you, I'm not in a position to deny it" and, oh … one thing strange. She said: "Some things one has to do, and only pray for forgiveness."'

Wycliffe took it on board and left Kersey and Lane to interview Lander again while he set off for Bottrell Hall. In the woods on the estate, he met Guy Bottrell who was organizing a paintball trail. The two men talked as they walked. Wycliffe came straight to the point. He wanted to know whether Guy had been involved with Lizzie Biddick.

Guy was not shy about his conquests. 'Okay, I did have a flirtation with the Biddick woman. But, believe me, I wasn't alone in that. Bit of a Delilah our Lizzie.'

'You had an affair?' asked Wycliffe, seeking confirmation.

'Did it a few times,' replied Guy with military brusqueness. 'Desperate men do desperate things. A rather dim tart, but a good body on her.'

'Mr Miller?'

'That's Hugh's department. I had nothing to do with that damn toilet loiterer.'

'And you were definitely with Lady Cynthia the night he died?'

'I realize being in bed with a lapful of one's brother's wife is not the choicest of alibis … but, *c'est la vie* … '

Wycliffe was not satisfied. 'Only Lady Cynthia was less specific when my colleague discussed the matter with her.'

Guy tried to shrug it off. 'Cynthia lives uneasily with her conscience. No doubt she's purged her guilt endlessly, done her Hail Marys … '

'You see, Mr Bottrell, I don't believe you were with her that night.'

'What?'

'I believe she's lying. To protect you.'

'Why? Why should she do that?'

'For the same reason she's suffered in silence all these years married to a man who doesn't, who can't, love her. "Keeping faith unto death". Isn't that the Bottrell family motto?'

Guy would not be shaken. 'I was with her.'

'And the night Lizzie Biddick died? Where were you then? Who were you with?'

'Er ... I don't know.'

'Somebody murdered Lizzie Biddick and dumped her body in a ditch, then went to her room, packed some things, slipped the photographs in the bag, hoping to implicate Mr Lander, and dumped the bag in a well, in these woods. You know that well?'

'Yes.'

'We will discover the truth, Mr Bottrell. We have fibres from the dead woman's fingernails. What were you wearing on the night of Lizzie Biddick's death? That sweater?'

'No!'

'What did you wear then?'

Guy had had enough. 'Look, she deserved everything she got. Yes ... all right. I killed her. But not before she'd killed me!'

'"Killed you?"' queried Wycliffe.

'She denied it, but I knew. She'd been at it with that queer, Miller. He was having it both ways.' Guy anticipated Wycliffe's next question. 'Yes. I disposed of him as well. One less piece of dross to worry about. He laughed at me. Denied he and she had ... I shoved the shotgun under his chin and ... '

At that, he fired a red paintball into the trunk of a tree. It splattered like the blood in Miller's cottage.

Guy Bottrell continued to try to justify his actions. 'Found out when I applied to renew my health insurance. Routine blood test they said, only I tested positive. HIV. It was her, the slut ... and him. They condemned me to a living death.' He added nobly: 'Any man would have done the same.'

However the post mortem on Lizzie Biddick told a different story. A routine blood test on her body proved negative. She was not HIV-positive. Neither was Miller. It transpired that Guy Bottrell had caught the HIV virus while stationed in the army in Kenya. He had killed twice for nothing.

'But then,' as Wycliffe said, 'the Bottrells are landed gentry. A law unto themselves. Always have been.'

THE SCAPEGOAT

Transmission date: 7 August 1994
Writer: Russell Lewis
Director: Martyn Friend

SUPPORTING CAST
Sarah Riddle - Carol Nimmons
Edith Riddle - Hilary Mason
Matthew Riddle - Alan Stocks
Mariah Penrose - Susan Penhaligon
Mr Penrose - Peter Stockbridge
Ephraim Gardner - John McEnery
Asenath Gardner
- Catherine McCormack
Sid Passmore - Stephen Tate
Sgt Luff - Christopher Ashley
WPC Eva Luff - Laura Brattan

Ephraim Gardner
(John McEnery, right)
leads the scapegoat
ceremony

It started out as a routine missing persons inquiry. Jonathan Riddle, building contractor and village undertaker, had disappeared a week earlier. He had last been seen by his family around seven-thirty on the Friday evening when he had gone back to his works' yard. His wife, Sarah, reported him missing two days later, on the Sunday evening. There was no particular reason to suspect that anything untoward had happened until a pile of clothes was discovered by children playing in a barn on Ephraim Gardner's farm. There was blood on the collar of the shirt. Mrs Riddle identified the clothing as that which her husband was last seen wearing. Wycliffe was called in.

It was obvious that something more sinister was afoot. 'If he was planning on going missing, I doubt he'd do it naked,' mused Wycliffe.

Local knowledge linked Riddle's disappearance to the Scapegoat ceremony, held each year on Midsummer's Eve and said to bring good luck to the village over the next twelve months by driving out all evil spirits. The ritual had been performed for centuries and was a spectacular affair. The Scapegoat, a wicker figure wearing a grotesque mask, was tied within a huge wheel, decorated with greenery and ribbons. At dawn, on a nearby headland, a number of villagers, attired like druids in white robes and head-dresses, approached the wheel, their leader carrying a staff. As torches were lit, the leader announced: 'This is the holy flame which shall consume our wickedness and purge our people of evil for the year to come.' The wheel was then set alight while onlookers chanted 'Burn! Burn! Burn!' Finally, at a signal from the leader, the blazing wheel was released to roll down the cliffs and plunge into the sea. According to legend, it was bad luck if the Scapegoat was ever washed up.

That year's ceremony took place on the Sunday following Jonathan Riddle's vanishing act. Wycliffe struggled to make a connection until the local bobby, Sergeant Luff, repeated a rumour he had heard.

'It's just folk getting daft ideas in their heads but one of the young girls at the ceremony – drunk, like as not – thought that as the wheel went bowling down towards the edge of the cliff that the mask, um, fell away, and it was, er, Riddle inside.'

'Anyone spring to mind who might have had it in for him?' asked Kersey.

'Not as you mean, sir,' replied Luff before giving the matter further consideration. 'Bit of bad blood between him and Ephraim Gardner.'

'About what?'

'Gardner's daughter, Asenath, had a kiddy about six months back. No father, see? None as'd give it a name leastways. Eph' got it into his head Riddle was responsible.'

'Why?' said Lane.

'She used to work up Riddle's yard, ma'am. I know it's a bag of nonsense, but he ain't been right since he lost his Missus. Not that he'd do anything mind. Bark's worse than his bite with Ephraim.'

Having set up an incident room at the local church hall, Wycliffe went off to talk to the missing man's wife. Three generations of Riddles lived in the house – Jonathan and Sarah, his mother Edith and their son Matthew who worked in the family business. It quickly became apparent that there was no love lost between Edith Riddle and her daughter-in-law. Sarah and Jonathan had argued that Friday evening about his insistence on going back to work after tea. It seemed that marital fall-outs were commonplace in the household. Edith blamed Sarah for the constant bickering.

'He worked bloody hard for you and Matthew,' she said bluntly, 'and all you could do was go on at him.'

'Shut up! Shut up! Shut up! You old witch,' blasted Sarah.

Wycliffe was glad he'd come. When the temperature cooled a little, he continued with his questioning.

'Had he stayed away before?'

'The odd night,' answered Sarah. 'He liked a drink.' She suddenly realized what she had said and corrected herself. 'Likes, I mean. He likes a drink.'

Wycliffe made a mental note of the slip. 'On the Saturday, you weren't worried when he didn't turn up?'

'I reckoned maybe he was after teaching me a lesson – staying away. It was the weekend. I said to Matthew, I said: "Your father's having a game with me." We laughed. No, I thought he might've gone to Frome. He's a friend out that way – from National Service. Drinking partner, you know.' She paused, hesitating to ask. 'Do you think ...?'

Edith completed the sentence. 'He's dead.'

Sarah was appalled at her insensitivity. 'Oh mother!'

'Why do you say that, Mrs Riddle?' said Wycliffe.

'I know my son,' said the old woman. 'He's never stopped away from home for any length of time. He'd've been into work Monday if he was able.'

It emerged that on that Friday, Jonathan Riddle had withdrawn the sum of £1,250 in cash from his building society account. He paid his workers in cash at the end of each week and usually drew out £1,000. But that day he had mysteriously requested the extra £250. His wallet, found with his clothing, had contained just £30.

Wycliffe tracked down Matthew Riddle, a dark-haired man of around thirty, in the Chapel of Rest at the family works. He had anticipated that it was one place where they would not be interrupted but no sooner had he ascertained that the business was not in any financial difficulties than a piercing scream was heard coming from the yard. Wycliffe and Matthew raced out to find Riddle's distraught secretary, Melanie, with Lane. The DI was holding a small box.

'Mr Riddle got a package Friday, sir,' said Lane. She opened the box to reveal a sheep's heart, seething with maggots. Pinned to the heart was a Tarot card – 'A Tower Struck Down'.

Meanwhile Kersey had discovered somebody else who had fallen out with Jonathan Riddle. Mixing business with pleasure in the village pub, Kersey was introduced to Sid Passmore, a weasel-like individual who sported a large earring in his right ear. A general tinker dealing in cars, he also ran a burger bar at a Wild West tourist attraction known as Frontier City out near St Columb Major. He and Jonathan Riddle had wanted to buy the same field but Passmore lost out when Riddle gazumped him. But he insisted that he bore no grudge.

Kersey also learned that at about 8pm on the Friday, an old man had spotted Jonathan Riddle heading out of the village on foot towards Westhead Point in the direction of Ephraim Gardner's farm.

'Gardner?' queried Wycliffe, sensing a development. 'Where his clothes were found?'

'Mmm,' concurred Kersey. 'Bloke's a complete nutter apparently. Fancies himself as a druid. He's the guy that organizes this Scapegoat thing.'

'Have a word,' said Wycliffe. 'See if Riddle came by his place Friday night.'

Just then Potter arrived to say that the remains of the wheel had been found washed up on the coast. There was no sign of the Scapegoat. Out at the scene, Wycliffe sought the benefit of Sergeant Luff's expertise.

'How was the Scapegoat attached to the wheel?'

'Tied, sir. Hands and feet.'

'With what?'

'Sash. Done up quite tight, I believe.'

'Who made it?'

'Ephraim Gardner.'

By then, Kersey was on his way to Gardner's farm. He approached the house but nobody appeared to be home. With a policeman's natural instinct, he nosed around inside. The walls were adorned with items pertaining to the occult. This was indeed a strange house. He decided to make the most of the opportunity and take a closer look. Suddenly, he gave a shudder as he felt cold metal pressing into his neck. It was the unmistakeable feel of the barrels of a shotgun. Ephraim Gardner had shown up.

The tall, gaunt figure of Gardner forced Kersey outside at gunpoint. Daughter Asenath appeared clutching her baby. Kersey protested that he was a police officer but Gardner wanted him off his land. Before the dispute could be resolved, Kersey swung round and elbowed Gardner in the eye. The gun went off, narrowly missing Asenath and the baby and shattering the windows on Kersey's car. At least he could claim back the damage on expenses.

Gardner, complete with black eye, was hauled in for questioning. Wycliffe had no doubt that it was Gardner who had sent the sheep's heart and tarot card to Jonathan Riddle. Not only did he have an unhealthy interest in the occult but he also had a motive since he seemed convinced that Riddle was the father of Asenath's baby. But Gardner would admit to nothing – least of all murder.

'Did Riddle come round to your house that particular Friday evening, Mr Gardner?' asked Wycliffe.

'No.'

'You sure about that?'

Gardner's response was silence.

Wycliffe was growing frustrated but it was not in his nature to let it show. 'All right. All right, let's talk about the wheel. Now I understand that you built the wheel yourself in one of your sheds? The shed where Riddle's clothes were found.'

Gardner seized on the implication. 'I told Sergeant Luff, I don't know how they got there.'

Wycliffe was prepared to give him the benefit of the doubt. 'The wheel was in there 'til when?'

'Saturday afternoon, the eve of the festival,' said Gardner.

'Would it have been possible for someone to get into your shed Friday night, remove the Scapegoat and substitute a body dressed in the Scapegoat's clothes?'

Gardner was not impressed by the theory. 'You don't want to listen to no gossip. People round here'll make up any old rubbish.'

'Could it have happened?' pressed Wycliffe.

'It could have – but it didn't.'

Wycliffe tried a different tack. 'Now the legend says it's bad luck if the Scapegoat washes up. That's right, isn't it?'

'The sea cleanses us of our sin.'

'But so far the Scapegoat's never been washed back up, has it?'

'It's bound tightly,' answered Gardner.

'Interesting bindings. Sash plaited with slow burning fuse. That's why your Scapegoat never came back, Mr Gardner.'

'Not yet, it hasn't, no.' Gardner leaned across the desk to speak in a hushed, almost eerie, tone. 'But this year... I had a dream. The Scapegoat was reaching up to me from the depths – pulling me down. His mouth was full of blood and he kissed me. I couldn't breathe. You mark my words, Mr Wycliffe, this year, he's coming back.'

Gardner's prophecy soon came true. The naked body of Jonathan Riddle was discovered lying on rocks at the foot of the cliffs. Police pathologist Dr Franks found five or six deep traumatic injuries to the skull but some, or all of these, could have been caused by the body being thrown against the rocks by the sea. The airways and lungs were waterlogged, and his estimate was that the body had been in the water at least six or seven days.

'Was he alive when he went in?' inquired Wycliffe.

'Well,' replied Franks, 'if it's seawater in his lungs then yes, he was. But I won't know that until the lab have done their sodium chloride test. That'll take a couple of days.'

'Any burns to wrists or ankles?'

Franks shook his head. 'No, the way things stand at the moment, he could either have been pushed off the top of a cliff – or simply walked into the sea of his own accord.' Franks also took great delight in volunteering the contents of the dead man's stomach – a meal of ham and tomatoes well on the way to being digested, several sherries, nuts, raisins and Turkish Delight. Wycliffe's expression belied his gratitude.

Wycliffe's first port of call was to check out Matthew Riddle's alibi for the Friday night. He said he had been to the pictures in Penzance, alone.

'What time did you get back home?' asked Wycliffe.

'It was late. The car had packed up on the way back. I went by Sid Passmore's about eleven-thirty. He was just back from Frontier City. So that was a bit of luck. He came back with me and got her started.'

Passmore confirmed the story, adding that he finally managed to get the car moving around two in the morning. Nevertheless Wycliffe still had his doubts about young Riddle, particularly when the accounts revealed that he had been swindling his father by over-ordering materials and selling off the surplus. The scam had been going on for the best part of a year and had netted Matthew a few thousand pounds, money he used to finance his gambling habit.

Wycliffe decided to clear his head by taking a stroll down to the rocks where Riddle's body was found. He noticed a water-filled basin and carefully studied its proximity to the sea. Then, gazing back at the house which overlooked the rocks, he spotted a figure with binoculars at an upstairs window. Approaching the house, he was met by the local schoolteacher, Mariah Penrose, an attractive woman in her early forties. She lived there with her invalid father. Now crippled with arthritis, he used to look after the sewage outfall by opening the sluice. For that reason, her father's room faced the sea while her own looked out on the footpath leading down to the rocks. Wycliffe wondered whether Jonathan Riddle might have passed that way on the Friday evening but Miss Penrose said she had seen nothing.

But the thinking time was not wasted. It enabled Wycliffe to draw some interesting conclusions as to who was the father of Asenath Gardner's baby. A visit to the farm confirmed his suspicions.

'Why have you been covering up for Matthew Riddle?' he asked Asenath.

The girl feigned ignorance.

'When did you tell him you were pregnant?' continued Wycliffe. 'About a year ago wasn't it? About the time he started stealing from his father.'

Asenath realized her secret was out but implored Wycliffe not to tell her father. Wycliffe assured her that whatever she said would remain strictly confidential.

'If Dad knew about Matthew, he'd want me to marry him.'

'Would that be such a bad thing?' inquired Wycliffe.

'God, I wouldn't marry Matthew if he was the last man on earth. I had it off with him, that's different.'

Although Wycliffe didn't approve, he understood.

'It happened when Dad went to Brittany – nine-day excursion. I was left here alone. I'd been out with Matthew once or twice, you know – Penzance, pictures.' She toyed with her long, straggly hair. 'With Dad away, that's when it happened.'

'You used to work at Riddle's yard, didn't you? Did Matthew ever talk to you about his father?'

'Like what?'

Wycliffe followed a hunch. 'How he got on with his wife?'

Asenath paused before delivering the bombshell. 'He had a woman.'

'Matthew told you that?'

'No. I worked that one out for myself. I went back to the office late one Friday. Riddle always made a big thing about working on the books of a Friday evening. Only he weren't there.'

'That's hardly...'

Asenath had further proof. 'And the johnnies. I found his johnnies.'

Sure enough, a search of Riddle's wardrobe at the Chapel of Rest uncovered a packet of condoms in the jacket pocket of his funeral suit.

'You think he had a mistress?' asked Lane.

Wycliffe eyed the body on the slab. 'Well, let's hope so.'

Sarah Riddle took the news badly. 'Filth! Filth! I won't hear such filth!' she shrieked. 'He didn't have to look elsewhere. He had me. I'd've done. He didn't have to...with that...Oh, I knew. Fridays...primping,

Something for the weekend, sir? Wycliffe politely declines.

preening, cutting the hairs in his nose. I could smell her on him. Sick! Sick! Love! You call that love? Like beasts…'

Suddenly she clutched her chest and slumped to the floor. She had suffered a heart attack. Wycliffe's attempts to ascertain the whereabouts of Mrs Riddle on the Friday night were interrupted by a report that Ephraim Gardner had been found dead at the farm with his throat cut. A self-penned note had been left in the kitchen. It read:

> 'Riddle came here last Friday as I asked him to. I let him sit down and then hit him on the back of the head with a brick. I took him down the Penrose place to the basin and put him in it. The sea did the rest. I am sorry for it and for what I have put Asenath through. I hope she can forgive me. Ephraim.'

Wycliffe was highly sceptical and his suspicions were borne out by Franks who immediately poured scorn on the suicide theory. 'Cut's in the right direction, left to right, but it's a single slice. Case like this you'd expect one or two tentative slashes before the real McCoy – not straight through the trachea first time. The slope's all wrong.'

'From the rear?' suggested Wycliffe.

'Like as not. SOCOs found something interesting about three feet behind him – some of a child's feed regurgitated.'

The implications horrified Wycliffe. Asenath had left her baby at the farm while she went down to the village. On her return, she had found her father's body. 'So you're saying…Oh dear God. You're saying Asenath's baby was set down over there? Which means what? His murderer threatens the baby. Ephraim writes the note. And the murderer comes all the way round, lays the baby down and cuts the man's throat.'

'Well, I leave the hypotheses to you, Charles,' replied Franks, 'but let's just say it's not an entirely discreditable scenario. Oh, by the way. Friend Riddle. Sodium chloride test. Turned out positive. Definitely seawater.'

Wycliffe decided to let the killer think he had fallen for the suicide note. In the meantime, he paid another call on Mariah

Penrose. On a table in her living room, he noticed a box of Turkish Delight and a bowl of nuts and raisins. He wasted no time in confronting her with the evidence.

She made no attempt to deny it. 'He was quite an educated man, you know. Well read. It wasn't the sex. That's the one people always assume, don't they? He wasn't fussed about the sex. Just wanted someone to talk to. To hold. To be held.'

'Did he come here every Friday night?'

'Almost – for the past two years – and Wednesdsays if he could.'

'What time did he arrive and leave the Friday before last?'

'He arrived just after eight-thirty and left around eleven.'

'What time did you go to bed that night?'

'Right after he left – around eleven-fifteen.'

Wycliffe walked over to the window. 'Tide's coming in.' He turned to Mariah. 'I'd like to speak to your father now.'

He found old Mr Penrose in his room overlooking the rocks where Riddle's body was discovered.

'Can you remember what the tide was like that Friday evening?'

'Was quiet. Misty rain. High tide was around eleven-fifteen. – about four, four and a half foot in the basin at the top of the flood.'

Wycliffe was in thoughtful mode. 'If a body was placed in the water at that time, would it have been washed away by the tide?'

'Unless it got snagged, certainly.'

'And if it was placed there later – say two o'clock?'

'There'd have been no water round the basin after one. Not enough to float a cork.'

'One last question, Mr Penrose. Could a body have been placed in the basin early Saturday morning and remained there until the next high tide without being seen?'

'Not a chance, sir.'

The pieces were beginning to fit together. Forensic reports on Riddle's clothing showed grass and mud deposits ground into the back of the jacket, shirt and trousers, suggesting that he had been dragged for some distance. Then Wycliffe received a message that Sarah Riddle wished to speak to him from her hospital bed. She knew that son Matthew was still under suspicion and wanted to clear his name.

'Matthew'd nothing to do with it,' she insisted.

'That's not strictly true, is it?' replied Wycliffe.

Sarah was adamant. 'It was me. I don't know how it happened, but...I can't remember...'

Wycliffe jogged her memory. 'You went out to Mariah Penrose's place? What time?'

'I slipped out of the house about half past nine. I'd left my car parked around the corner.'

Wycliffe was sympathetic. 'What happened, Sarah?'

'I don't know. Had enough, I suppose. I just wanted to see the look on his face. I waited for him 'til he came out. Just after eleven.' Her voice became more animated. 'Kissing her on the porch. Putting his tongue in her mouth. Something went in me. She went back inside and he came over towards the road. It was the car he recognized.'

'Where were you?'

'Round the side of the house. I found I had a rock in my hand. I ran up behind him and hit him on the back of the head. He fell down and ... I don't remember...'

'And then what did you do?'

'I went home and had a bath.'

'Why did you send Matthew up there? If you're going to tell it, you might as well tell it all.'

'Matthew.' The words stuck in her throat. 'Matthew was just...He was just being kind. He's a good boy.'

'What time was this?'

'About one, he got back from Penzance. He said he'd tidied up.'

Matthew was hauled in for questioning.

'What did you offer Sid Passmore?' asked Wycliffe.

'I promised him he could come in on the business. His stall ain't doing so well.'

'That was very generous of you', said Wycliffe sardonically.

'What could I do? It was my mum.'

'Why'd you go to him in the first place? Couldn't you manage the body alone?'

'Why'd I go to him? I never. He was there when I arrived. He saw what happened and got the body off the road down to the basin.'

'But the tide was going out.'

'Was no way Dad was going to float off. So we dragged him back again.'

'He was dead?'

'Yes. Mum had – you saw him. It wasn't only the cliffs that did that to his head.'

'So, on Saturday with everyone up at the Scapegoating, you and Passmore decided to give it another go.'

'Yeah. I never knew what he'd done with the clothes – putting them on Ephraim's land. None of that.'

'What did you do with your father?'

'I'd brung a bodybag from work. I put him in that and we stuck him in the boot of the car. I drove back to the yard and hid him there, in one of the caskets, 'til the following evening.' He looked Wycliffe straight in the eye. 'I never touched him, Mr Wycliffe. I just tried to cover up what my mum'd done.'

Wycliffe believed Matthew was being honest with him but there remained the matter of the seawater in Riddle's lungs. Sid Passmore was cooking behind the bar of the saloon at Frontier City when Wycliffe, Kersey and Lane paid him a visit. He soon realized they were not there for the burgers.

'I never done nothing,' protested Passmore. 'I was just helping Matthew out.'

Wycliffe was not fooled. 'You murdered Ephraim Gardner and Jonathan Riddle.'

'No.'

'You know what sodium chloride is, Mr Passmore?' He picked up a salt pot from the counter. 'Salt. Common salt. The difference between freshwater and seawater. And it was seawater we found in Jonathan Riddle's lungs. He was still breathing when you put him in the basin. Dying, perhaps, but you drowned him. You knew there was no love lost between Riddle and Gardner, didn't you? That's why you hid the clothes on his land.'

'I never. I was helping Matthew out.'

'You'd been watching Riddle. Looking for some way to pay him back for gazumping you.'

'You're barmy!'

Wycliffe persisted. 'By attacking Riddle, Sarah gave you more than you could have wanted. You played the concerned friend for all it was worth. And when you thought we might crack Matthew or his mother, you murdered Gardner and then tried to make it look like suicide. He was your Scapegoat.'

By now, Passmore was desperate. Saying he had to turn the gas off, he reached under the counter just as Sgt Luff entered the saloon. Luff saw what he was really up to and shouted: 'Gun!'

Passmore fired at Luff, wounding him in the shoulder, and

Sid Passmore (Stephen Tate) ready for the showdown

made his escape. Kersey chased after him while Wycliffe tried to clear the street of tourists before there was a real shoot-out. Passmore fired off two shots at Kersey, hitting a barrel then a window. Kersey attempted to talk him into giving himself up but Passmore simply reloaded and pointed the shotgun straight at Kersey's head. He was about to shoot when Wycliffe appeared to his left, brandishing a pistol.

'Armed police!' yelled Wycliffe. 'Put that weapon down! You pull that trigger and I'll shoot. Go on, drop it! Do it! Now!'

Passmore momentarily glanced towards Wycliffe but that was all Kersey needed to rush in and overpower him, knocking the shotgun out of his hands. With Passmore immobilized, Wycliffe calmly handed the pistol back to one of the Frontier City bandits from whom he had borrowed it. It was only a replica. Passmore had been out-witted by the coolest *hombre* in town.

THE TANGLED WEB

While Elinor Clemo was being buried, at nearby Tregelles Farm the body of her sister, Agnes Rule, was found in a freezer. Agnes had lived there with her sister-in-law, Jane Rule, and Jane's backward son Clifford. The latter, who had a previous conviction for actual bodily harm after an incident outside a girls' school in Tregavissey, immediately did a runner when he saw Wycliffe and the team arriving at the farm. In the course of his investigations into the circumstances surrounding Agnes's death, Wycliffe heard rumours about a valuable painting which had once been hanging on the wall of Agnes's bedroom. It had gone missing and Wycliffe was told that Agnes's niece, Hilda Clemo, who had identified it as a genuine Pissarro, would be able to tell him about it. Unfortunately, Hilda too had gone missing following a row with her boyfriend Ralph. She had informed him that she was pregnant but had no intention of having an abortion. Ralph insisted that he had last seen her at Porthellis waiting to catch the bus home. The head of the Clemo family, James, knew of Hilda's pregnancy. He ran a profitable caravan park, the site manager of which was his son-in-law Francis Harvey. As well as renting out a cottage to the Rules, James Clemo's other tenants were a married couple, Neil and Polly Innes. He was a teacher and she was a wheelchair-bound artist. That night, Harvey and wife Alice searched the area around Tregelles Farm and found Hilda's bloodstained trainer. There was still no sign of Clifford and his mother was proving less than helpful. As the search for Hilda intensified, Ralph was forced to concede that he had not left her at Porthellis but had argued with her near Tregelles Farm. Wycliffe and Kersey visited Neil and Polly Innes, having learned that Hilda was a regular visitor to their house. According to Mr Innes, she went there for tuition. He added that he had seen her at three o'clock the previous afternoon (a Sunday) near a local

Transmission date:
14 August 1994
Writer: Andrew Holden
Director: Ferdinand Fairfax

SUPPORTING CAST
Jane Rule - Richenda Carey
Clifford Rule - Giles Taylor
Francis Harvey - Kevin Dignam
Hilda Clemo - Stephanie Buttle
Lily Armitage - Gabrielle Hamilton
Ralph Martin - Scott Ransome
James Clemo - Robert Demeger
Alice Clemo - Jo Thirsk
Neil Innes - Eric Deacon
Polly Innes - Leonie Mellinger

There is more to Polly Innes (Leonie Mellinger) than meets the eye

The police discover the
body of Hilda Clemo

quarry. Kersey left convinced that Innes and Hilda were an item. Details began to emerge of a family rift about furniture and the aforementioned painting. Indeed Hilda had written to the National Gallery last year in an attempt to ascertain the value of the painting. Agnes and Elinor's late brother Henry had dealt in antiques. His will had stipulated that all the contents of his house, including the painting, should be left to the surviving sister. If Agnes were to die first, it would go to the Clemos but if Elinor were to die first, it would go to Jane Rule and her family. Clifford Rule was finally arrested. He said he had run away in panic because he was scared of the police (his conviction for assault had been for striking a policeman). The pathology report stated that Agnes had died of natural causes – from a brain haemorrhage. Wycliffe began to unravel the tangled web of intrigue. Jane Rule had immediately placed Agnes's body in the freezer, hoping to conceal her death until Elinor Clemo passed away. Thus Jane would inherit the painting which Hilda had estimated as being worth £500,000. Hilda had tried to persuade Agnes to give the painting to her and not Jane. The day after her disappearance, the body of Hilda Clemo was found by police frogmen in the water-filled quarry. She had been battered around the head with a small hammer. Under interrogation, Francis Harvey confessed that Hilda had been sleeping with Neil Innes for about two years – since she was fifteen. He had loaned Innes his caravan for their personal use and added that he had seen Hilda at half past three on the Sunday afternoon going into Innes's cottage. Innes admitted that he and Hilda had been lovers and that he had murdered her and dumped her in the quarry. But Wycliffe knew better. The killer was Mrs Innes. She had heard that Hilda was pregnant and feared that she would lose her husband to the girl. The irony was that Hilda had never been pregnant at all. It had just been a ploy to get her man. But it had cost her her life.

THE LAST RITES

Walking down the aisle to the altar of his church early one Sunday morning, Rev. Michael Jordan stumbled across the dead body of cleaner Jessica Dobell, spreadeagled at the feet of Jesus and next to a plaque which read: 'The soul that sinneth, it shall die – Ezekiel 18, 4'. She had been felled by a sharp blow to the head and, although her clothing had been partly removed, there had been no sexual assault. She had been dragged to her final resting place. The dead woman's sister, Katherine, was married to Abe Geach. The Geaches lived at the Old Vicarage next to the church while Jessica lived at a nearby farm where her tenants were a family called the Vinters. Rev. Jordan, who had arrived at church earlier than usual that day in order to collect his sheet music, gave organ lessons to the Vinters' son Giles. There was little love lost between Miss Dobell and Lawrence and Stephanie Vinter. The Geaches would now inherit the farm and the Vinters were expecting to be evicted any day. Katherine Geach revealed that Jessica was considering throwing the Vinters out anyway and added that she herself had argued with her sister on the evening of her death. She had last seen Jessica alive at 8.15pm. A picture of the dead woman began to emerge. She was not popular with the locals, being a firm believer in sex rather than religion. Her morals had met with considerable disapproval and she had been the recipient of some rather unpleasant letters. In particular, she had incurred the wrath of Rev. Jordan's sister Celia, President of the Christian Women's Union. The Secretary of the same union was Stephanie Vinter. Wycliffe was puzzled by the absence of the sheet music. Rev. Jordan had been to collect it that morning but had abandoned his plans on discovering the body. So why wasn't the music still in the church? Franks disclosed that Jessica Dobell was pregnant at the time of her death and that in the back pocket of her skirt was another unsavoury letter – the fourth in all – still unopened. The note read: 'These shall hate the whore and shall make her desolate and naked and devour her

Transmission date:
21 August 1994
Writer: Rob Heyland
Director: A.J.Quinn

SUPPORTING CAST
Lawrence Vinter - Nigel Terry
Stephanie Vinter - Julia Deakin
Katherine Geach - Ellie Haddington
Abe Geach - Paul Moriarty
Rev. Jordan - Jeff Rawle
Celia Jordan - Dinah Stabb
Giles Vinter - Mark Letheren
Glynn - Geoffrey Leesley

flesh and burn her up like fire.' Celia Jordan admitted having sent the first three letters but not the fourth. Meanwhile Abe Geach said he had seen Jessica at 9pm on the evening of her death. She was polishing the altar rail of the church. He also confessed to having had an affair with his sister-in-law but denied emphatically that he was the father of her child. That prerogative, he said, belonged to Lawrence Vinter. Giles Vinter, a precocious youth, casually mentioned that his father had stayed out on the night of the murder. Giles had been to the church for an organ lesson that evening but had not collected the sheet music. Rev. Jordan, who appeared to be extremely close to Giles, said that, as a result of a huge family row over his father's affair, Giles had been very upset the night Jessica Dobell was killed. He had comforted the boy by putting his arm around him, just as Miss Dobell walked into church. Jessica had made a great play of their embarrassment, causing Giles even greater distress. Lawrence contemplated suicide but Wycliffe caught up with him and he confessed to the murder. However Wycliffe knew he was covering up for someone. For when Vinter had gone into the church that night, he had seen Giles standing over the body of Jessica Dobell. He had attempted to hide the incriminating evidence but had made the mistake of removing the sheet music, believing that it belonged to Giles when in fact it was the property of Rev. Jordan. Giles had killed Jessica to stop her spreading rumours about him and Rev. Jordan. And Lawrence had tried to protect a boy who held him in utter contempt.

Wycliffe and Lane seek spiritual guidance

THE PEA GREEN BOAT

Garage proprietor Harry Tremaine was out fishing in his boat *The Green Bounty* when it suddenly exploded. Harry was found dead, washed up in a rock pool, and his thirty-two-year-old son Freddie, also thought to be on board, was declared missing presumed dead. The explosion appeared to have been deliberate. At Harry's garage, one of the mechanics, David Jones, revealed that Freddie had been dipping his fingers in the till to finance his extravagant lifestyle. It also began to seem highly unlikely that Freddie had been on the boat at the time of the explosion. The luckiest man around was Alex Greaves, half-owner of *The Green Bounty.* He would normally have been out on the boat on the fateful day but had been sidelined by flu. Freddie's ex-wife, Mary, lived with Bill Clark who worked at the quarry from where a quantity of explosives had gone missing. Clark also had form for petty theft but Mary suggested that a more likely culprit was Freddie. He had often talked about scuppering the boat as an insurance job. Freddie was indeed still alive and was arrested pursuing one of his favourite interests – banger car racing. He claimed to have been in Truro on the night before the explosion but couldn't come up with any witnesses to support his story. Lane learned from Mrs Tremaine that Harry and Alex Greaves

Transmission date:
28 August 1994
Writer: Steve Trafford
Director: A.J.Quinn

SUPPORTING CAST
Harry Tremaine - Roy Alon
Mrs Tremaine - Anne Stallybrass
Freddie Tremaine - David Westhead
David Jones - Brendan O'Hea
Mary Clark - Jan Pearson
Bill Clark - Tony Guilefoyle
Alexander Greaves - Barry Jackson
Ian Greaves - Paul Bettany
Ella Jones - Brigit Forsyth
Garner - Kevin Molloy
Forbes - Emmett Bergin

The Green Bounty explodes, killing Harry Tremaine

Ian and Alex Greaves
(Paul Bettany and
Barry Jackson)

had been offered a lot of money by property developer Daniel Forbes to sell their harbourside fish sheds to make way for a new marina, but Harry had steadfastly refused to sell up. The terms of the deeds stated that on the decease of either partner, disposal of the property reverted to the survivor. Harry's will left everything to his wife and Freddie, apart from £20,000 to the Bethesda Chapel where he was a lay preacher. His bank statements showed that he made all his transactions through his local branch except on the first of every month when he went to the bank in Truro and drew out £500 in cash. At Freddie's flat, Lane, Potter and Dixon found bomb-making equipment – the type that had wrecked the boat. Freddie owed a sizeable sum of money to Daniel Forbes – gambling debts – but denied blackmailing his father. He did however tell Wycliffe that his mother had been having an affair with Alex Greaves for years. It soon emerged that Harry had been keeping a secret of his own. The monthly £500 was paid to Ella Jones, a stalwart of the Bethesda Chapel, and mother of David. Harry was David's father. Ella had never told the boy. Harry had paid for him to go through university where David had studied chemistry. Alarm bells began to ring in Wycliffe's head. He, Kersey and Lane set off on a dramatic pursuit of David Jones which only ended when Jones's car swerved off the road and came to rest at the edge of a cliff. Wycliffe approached him gingerly. David remained inside the car, perched perilously on the brink. He said that he had known for years that Harry was his father – he had discovered letters. But Harry had always denied it and had threatened to sack him if he breathed a word of it to anyone. What further upset David was that Freddie, a complete waste of space, stood to inherit everything. So David tried to ruin them both. He blew up the boat and planted the incriminating chemicals in Freddie's flat. Wycliffe endeavoured to persuade David to step out of the car and give himself up but instead David released the handbrake and the car plunged over the cliff and exploded on impact on the beach below. Freddie Tremaine was free to go.